THE

MAKER
MOVEMENT
MANIFESTO

RULES FOR INNOVATION
IN THE NEW WORLD OF
CRAFTERS, HACKERS, AND TINKERERS

MARK HATCH

New Lenox
Public Library District
120 Veterans Parkway
New Lenox, Illinois 60451

Mc Graw Hill Education

New York   Chicago   San Francisco   Athens   London   Madrid
Mexico City   Milan   New Delhi   Singapore   Sydney   Toronto

1 2 3 4 5 6 7 8 9 0   DOC/DOC   1 8 7 6 5 4 3

ISBN: 978-0-07-182112-4
MHID: 0-07-182112-0

e-ISBN: 978-0-07-182113-1
e-MHID: 0-07-182113-7

Library of Congress Cataloging-in-Publication Data

Hatch, Mark, 1960-
 The maker movement manifesto : rules for innovation in the new world of crafters, hackers, and tinkerers / by Mark Hatch.
     pages cm
  ISBN-13: 978-0-07-182112-4 (alk. paper)
  ISBN-10: 0-07-182112-0 (alk. paper)
  1. Diffusion of innovations--Economic aspects. 2. Technological innovations--Economic aspects. I. Title.
  HC79.T4H368 2014
  658.4'063--dc23   2013017764

McGraw-Hill books are available at special quantity discounts to use as premiums and sales promotions, or for use in corporate training programs. To contact a representative, please visit the Contact Us page at www.mhprofessional.com.

Contents

■ ■ ■

Acknowledgments

First to Jim Newton, thank you for inviting me to join you on this amazing adventure. Then to our biggest partners: Autodesk, Ford, DARPA, the VA, Lowe's, and GE, thank you for believing. This includes a large part of Autodesk's executive team, Carl Bass, Jeff Kowalski, Chris Bradshaw, Amar Hanspal, Samir Hanna, Mark Hawkins, "Buzz" Kross, and Steve Blum. Others at Autodesk have been instrumental, including Sean James, Josh Ewing, Jon Pitman, Jonathan Knowles, Maurice Conti, Gonzalo Martinez, Tom Wujec, Jesse Au, Mike Guyer, Mary Hope McQuiston, and, of course, Brian Pene. All of them have helped the Maker Movement, TechShop, and I in specific ways. Thank you also to the chain of folks that got us to Autodesk, Paul Saffo and Chuck House.

To Ford and its employees, including Bill Ford III, Bill Coughlin, Charles Ericson, Venkatesh Prasad, Paul Mascarenas, Randal Visintainer, Alan Hall, John Ellis, David Evans, T.J. Giuli, and Janet Wilson, I express my appreciation. Ford helped to validate our model and through it gave a great boost to the movement.

DARPA and the VA have been great partners, already bringing TechShop to Pittsburgh to thousands of veterans across the United States. You know who you are.

The Lowe's team has leaned into this area with great enthusiasm. To the team including Jay Rebello, Jim Piazza,

Chris Stigliano, and Jonathan Luster—you made our pilot outside of Austin, Texas, a reality . . . an amazing reality actually. When giving tours of our space there, I say, "And on the other side of this door is our 110,000-square-foot retail space operated by our partner Lowe's. If you need anything, that is the best place to start."

Thank you to our staff, current, former, and future. You make this possible. I will call out Robert Thomas (a cofounder), Sesame Mish, Dan Woods (a cofounder of Make: magazine and this whole movement), Carrie Motamedi, Joe Menard, Dan Gonzales, Abe Downey, Derek Yu, Mark Dehner, Scott Saxon, Will Brick, Vance Hatch, Mike Catterlin, Paul Duggan, Jim Robinson, Rick Taylor, Clay Lambert, Matt Verlinich, Terry Sandin, Tackett Austin, Les Giles, Russ Stanphill, Cadence Shae, Laurie Connolly, Curtis C, Centa Schumacher, Denney Cole, Parts, Noah Chittim, Carmen Dalalo, Patrick Taylor, Myles Cunningham, Christina DeAngelo, Christopher Gangai, Joshua Handel, Michelle La Chance, Justin Leathers, Marie Lo, Jessica Marzetta, Thomas McIntosh, Gregori Niculitcheff, Chris Sasek, Robert Slack, Brian Ward, Rory Ward, Jennifer Benitez, Michael Budner, Emily Crocker, Cody Culbertson, Blain Dehmlow, Daniel Garcia, Hohammed Ghaymouni, Hassam Samimifar, Aaron Haldiman, Jarod Holtz, Angie Hsu, James Irmiger, Cory Jarman, Zachary Johnson, Ryan Lambert, Conor Landenberger, Athony Litwak, Ivan Lopez, Juan Mantez, Sean McBride, Kyle Moore, Claude Noriega, Mel Olivares, Gustavo Pastre, Violet Riggs, Alberto Salinas, Matthew Schutte, Ryan Spurlock, Elle Stapleton, Laura Stevenson, Matthew Stollenwerk, Ryan Acks, Justin Bell, Andrew Brandt, Raphael Colet, Eva Cooper, Karen Davis, J Duclayan, Robert Hanson, Laura Henry, Colin Jaramillo, Kacey Kvamme, Erik Ludwig, Bradley Martinson, Cody McCabe, Eric Munoz, Moraia Norman, Mike O'Connell,

Michelle Romero, Ian Thorp, Nicolas Valverde, Andrew Wong, Scott Berels, Jason Burton, Jodi Burton, Carly DeCocker, Lesley DiPiazza, Jamie Goforth, Aaron Keast, Taylor Kurrle, Steven Kuypers, Joshua Mathieu, Neill Odenwald, Andrea Oleniczak, Faith Olson, Rebekka Parker, Shawn Simone, Elizabeth Teifer, Cristopher Bessent, Brittnie Dilley, Kathryn Lynn Hange, Carl Johnson, Sara Kali, Jessica Renee Kliewer, Christopher Mahler, Christian Manrodt, Karen Nallie, Logan Pelafigue, Richard Simmons, Bess Siritanapivat, Samuel Spetalnick, Erik Withers, Alixis Rosa Caldero, Gabriel Cottrell, Timonth Currence, Kathryn Kelly, Joseph Gies, Cheyenne Grimes, Andrew Leer, Gadsen Merrill, Lucas Nene, Chloe Newman, Anthony Olivieri, Jordan Patton, Kathryn Rose, Elizabeth Solomon, Toyer Alexander, David White.

Designer extraordinaire Nambi Gardner and her cohorts Laura Cresciamano and Brenden Mendoza, helped make the San Francisco location and then the follow-on locations wonderful. Fellow Green Beret and general contractor Bill Lloyd, along with his wife Maria and sons Nick, Tristan, and Marcus, have been friends and now collaborators for 30 years. Thanks also to our finance team, including David Ehrenburg, Dee and Mike Hibberd, Fern Heyman, and Rosemary Vo for all your hard work.

We have a great group of advisers who have helped TechShop and me in various ways: Doug Busch (board member), Chris Anderson, Guy Kawasaki, Nolan Bushnel, Eric Von Hippel, Joe Pine, Jerry Gramaglia, Bruce Wonnacott, Todd Ordal, and Phoenix Wang.

Thank you to all the "friends of TechShop" like Bob Johanson, Mickey McManus, the Make Magazine crew, North of Nine Communications, our friends at Singularity University, Lesa Mitchel at Kauffman, Ping Fu, Nick Pinkston, James McKelvy, Patrick Buckley, Jane Chen, Taylor Kuffner,

Patrick Maloney, Bre Pettis, Ayah Bdeir, Logan McClore, Frank Piler, Loren Kennedy, Liam Casey, Lisa Gansky, Niels Neilsen, Deborah Cullinan, Mary Sullivan, Mike Rowe, Jeff Kempler, Michael Ventura, Mike North, Vivek Wadhwa, Anton Willis, Jennifer Giering, our Forest City friends including Alexa Arena, Alex Michel and Kevin Ratner, Dave Byers at Hearst, Scott Bohannon, all of our investors, lenders and members.

A shout out to the team that pulled this together: Laurie Connolly again, who cleaned up my scribbling before the editors got to see it; my agent Frank Breeden (thanks for hanging in there); Donya Dickerson without whom this book would not be in your hands; and Pamela Peterson, Chelsea Van Der Gaag, Scott Kurtz, and a host of others who help sell, market, and ship.

To my wife and life partner Cindy and our two great boys, Christopher and Luke, thank you for doing life with me.

Maker Movement Manifesto

MAKE

Making is fundamental to what it means to be human. We must make, create, and express ourselves to feel whole. There is something unique about making physical things. These things are like little pieces of us and seem to embody portions of our souls.

SHARE

Sharing what you have made and what you know about making with others is the method by which a maker's feeling of wholeness is achieved. You cannot make and not share.

GIVE

There are few things more selfless and satisfying than giving away something you have made. The act of making puts a small piece of you in the object. Giving that to someone else is like giving someone a small piece of yourself. Such things are often the most cherished items we possess.

LEARN

You must learn to make. You must always seek to learn more about your making. You may become a journeyman or master craftsman, but you will still learn, want to learn, and push yourself to learn new techniques, materials, and processes. Building a lifelong learning path ensures a rich and rewarding making life and, importantly, enables one to share.

TOOL UP

You must have access to the right tools for the project at hand. Invest in and develop local access to the tools you need to do the making you want to do. The tools of making have never been cheaper, easier to use, or more powerful.

PLAY

Be playful with what you are making, and you will be surprised, excited, and proud of what you discover.

PARTICIPATE

Join the Maker Movement and reach out to those around you who are discovering the joy of making. Hold seminars, parties, events, maker days, fairs, expos, classes, and dinners with and for the other makers in your community.

SUPPORT

This is a movement, and it requires emotional, intellectual, financial, political, and institutional support. The best hope for improving the world is us, and we are responsible for making a better future.

CHANGE

Embrace the change that will naturally occur as you go through your maker journey. Since making is fundamental to what it means to be human, you will become a more complete version of you as you make.

In the spirit of making, I strongly suggest that you take this manifesto, make changes to it, and make it your own. That is the point of making.

Introduction

Welcome to the next big thing, the Maker Movement and its revolution. We are still riding out the waves of the last big things, the computer revolution and the explosion of the Internet. But because the maker revolution is physical, it is destined to be bigger. We can't live in a computer or on the Internet, but we do live in houses, drive cars, wear clothes, use medical devices, play with toys, eat, grow, and live in the real world. I love the virtual world, but even its next big foray—the Internet of Things (where we connect physical objects up to sensors attached to the Internet)—will leverage and reside in its very physicalness. For the Internet of Things to work, there must be "things" to be attached to. What is happening and helping to drive the Maker Movement is that the nature of making things is changing. That is primarily what this book is about: the changing nature of making things and its tremendous impact on your life.

TECHSHOP, INC.

I'm the CEO of TechShop, a membership-based, do-it-yourself (DIY), open access, fabrication workspace. From my unique perch in the Maker community, I have had the opportunity over the last six years to see the emergence of a movement, the Maker Movement. TechShop is an integral player in that movement. Started in October 2006 by Jim Newton and a group of diehard maker enthusiasts in Menlo Park, California, TechShop was the first open-access shop of its kind. With six locations open across the United States at the time of this writing, and many more in the works and aspirations to go international, TechShop is now the largest and most influential makerspace in the world.

Shop locations average 16,000 to 20,000 square feet in size, with every tool and piece of equipment needed to make just about anything . . . like the world's fastest motorcycle, the world's first desktop diamond-manufacturing device, the world's cheapest drip irrigation system, and award-winning start-ups, one of which is currently worth billions of dollars. It is the most creative hub of activity in every city where it opens. People move to be near one; others take extended vacations in them; and a number of venture-backed start-ups have temporarily relocated their engineering teams to work out of the space. TechShop is changing the nature of making things, who gets to make them, and how they are made. The platform is allowing anyone over 16 years old to make almost anything, in a space designed for them, with access to the world's most powerful and easy-to-use machines the world has ever seen.

A LITTLE ABOUT ME

Through my work at Avery Dennison in the 1990s as corporate director of global technology and business development, I developed an understanding of the importance of and barriers to manufacturing. As director of computer services at Kinko's at the beginning the 2000s, where I managed a $200-million product line of publically available, open access, computers systems (10,000+) along with powerful software tied to large expensive high production machines, I saw firsthand the transformative power of open access to tools. We launched more design firms every year out of Kinko's than any school ever did.

As the former owner/operator of an auto body shop, I understand the importance of pride and craftsmanship, the local aversion to manufacturing, and the sometimes stifling effects of regulation. And now, as the CEO of TechShop, I have a unique opportunity to arm a Maker Movement army with the tools it needs to change itself and the world.

Along the way, I also picked up an MBA at the feet of the grandfather of management, Peter Drucker, and I am a trained revolutionary, thanks to the Special Forces training I received on my way to becoming a Green Beret. I use the dialectic of movements, manifestos, and revolutions explicitly.

MAKER MOVEMENT MOMENTUM

A number of trends are coming together to push the Maker Movement forward. Cheap, powerful, and easy-to-use tools play an important role. Easier access to knowledge, capital, and markets also help to push the revolution. A renewed focus on community and local resources and a desire for more authentic and quality things, along with a renewed interest in how to make things, also contribute to the movement. I'll cover each in its own way, but with a multiplicity of trends pushing along the Maker Movement, we have only begun to see an outline of its eventual power to remake the United States and the world.

The founders of this movement launched *Make Magazine*, the bible of the Maker Movement, in January 2005. Dale Dougherty, Sherry Huss, and Dan Woods, along with the support and encouragement from Tim O'Reilly, launched the magazine and then the Maker Faire, an annual gathering of 50,000 to 125,000 in three major cities around the country,

Modeled after the old *Popular Mechanics* format, with a heavy emphasis on describing projects that could be made by the home enthusiast, *Make Magazine* has become the touchstone of the movement. The arrival of each magazine is like getting a new Christmas catalog of things you want . . . to make.

When the group launched the first Maker Faire in San Mateo, California, in April 2006, 25,000 people showed up, many from out of state, wanting to connect with other people like themselves. And just like that, with an eclectic mix of people, projects, and things, the twenty-first-century version of the state fair was born. Eight years later, with expansions to hundreds of Mini Maker Faires in other cities and states around the country, the San Mateo Maker Faire will likely top 125,000 visitors and participants in 2013. With its annual draw of tens of thousands of acolytes joining together to celebrate making things, Maker Faire is like Mecca to the Maker Movement.

At the first Faire, future TechShop founder Jim Newton sat with a table, a sign, and an idea. By October 2006, he, his partner, and a bunch of volunteers had opened the first full-blown makerspace.

Since then, the movement has begun, and TechShop has been joined by many other companies. We have partnered with Autodesk, the software company that owns AutoCAD, Inventor, 3ds Max, and Maya. Autodesk has jumped into the Maker Movement with both feet, releasing a slew of free software, making it possible for anyone eight to eighty to design and make. The company has also increased its pace of acquisitions with purchases like Instructables.com, an online free instructional website where one can learn and share how to make almost anything.

Ford Motor Company, DARPA, the Veterans Administration, General Electric, Lowe's Home Improvement, National Instruments, and a growing number of other large and small companies have recently joined with us and others in helping to drive the message, platforms, and impact of this movement.

New companies have emerged as a result of the Maker Movement. AdaFruit, Sparkfun, Inventibles, Quirky, and MakerBot Industries all come to mind. One of the keys to this movement is the democratizing impact of access to the tools one needs to make things.

I met Jim Newton, founder and now chairman of TechShop, at a software party in Palo Alto, California, in 2007. I overheard him describe the workshop as being "kind of like Kinko's for geeks." Since, at one point in my career, I had run the geekiest part of Kinko's (the computer services area across the United States), I was intrigued. I thought to myself, "I am Kinko's for geeks. What is this guy talking about?" Eventually, Jim got me to come and take a look at the first TechShop location in Menlo Park, and he introduced me to the beginning of the movement.

At one point on that first visit, I went from table to table in the store asking, "What are you making?" Three times in a row I talked to entrepreneurs who told me that they had saved 95–98 percent of their development costs by using TechShop to make their initial products and sometimes their first couple of production runs.

I had done plenty of business development, product development, new product, or service launches along with research and development in my career. A 98 percent reduction in the cost of launching a product or company means, for example, that what used to cost $100,000 now costs just $2,000. This is stunning. It moves something from being hard or impossible to easily doable by anyone in the middle class. This platform democratizes hardware innovation in one fell swoop.

Jim showed me the class infrastructure and educational track that could be taken by anyone and that would move each person from not knowing how to make anything to helping him or her become a confident maker. And then I met the TechShop members. This was the most amazing group of artists, scientists, entrepreneurs, students, crafters, investors, and engineers I had ever encountered in one location. Some of them were already on a path to change the world. I was instantly hooked—and you will be too. You will meet many of these people in the following pages.

These have been six of the most amazing years of my life. I've met the most interesting, innovative, optimistic, energetic, and engaging men, women, and kids one can imagine. Many of my heroes have become friends, and many of my new friends have become heroes of the movement.

When I first started this journey, I believed that if this Maker Movement could scale up, it could actually impact the world in a positive manner. Six years later, I don't just believe this anymore . . . I know it. I have proof. Our members have changed the world in significant ways. Important companies have launched out of our space and the movement at large.

You will have to read the book to learn more, but what I know now is that we are at just the beginning of the largest explosion of creativity and innovation the world has ever seen. I know that these platforms revolutionize innovation in a way the world has never before seen. I know that the Maker way, thought, and movement will become a defining characteristic of at least the first half of this century, if not most of it. I know this because I see it play out every day in my role as the CEO of TechShop. I get to see people pursue their dreams of changing the world . . . and then watch them and others do it again and again and again. I get to interact with our staff members, who tell me they have a hard time believing all the amazing things our members are doing and making. They tell me that being a part of this makerspace is the most interesting, fun, and meaningful work they have ever had.

I get to host dignitaries, futurists, consultants, and exploratory committees that come to the Silicon Valley to see the next big thing and try to understand how they might be able to take some of the great ideas home.

Please forgive me for talking about TechShop throughout the book. I use the generic "makerspace" wherever I can, where it makes sense, and where it doesn't detract from the facts. But we have the leading makerspace in the market with six locations spread across the United States today. We have become one of the leading brands in this emerging market. The point of this book is not to shill for TechShop. Rather, it is to shine a light on what will become one of the most important movements of a generation, and then to invite *you* to participate in it.

I became a Green Beret years ago and adopted the motto, "De Oppresso Liber." This translates as "to liberate the oppressed." Little did I know at the time that the real opportunity for me to help "liberate the oppressed" would come through helping TechShop achieve its goal of democratizing access to the tools of the next industrial revolution. It has been an amazing ride so far and promises to become even more amazing as the movement grows in the United States and then around the world. This movement will not stop at the U.S. borders. It is too fundamental. It will eventually wash over the entire world.

I was thrilled recently when Chris Anderson, formerly of *Wired* magazine (the preeminent chronicler of all things web-related), told an audience filled with his peers that, "If you thought the web was big, I think this is going to be bigger."

I couldn't agree more.

The real power of this revolution is its democratizing effects. Now, almost anyone can innovate. Now, almost anyone can make. Now, with the tools available at a makerspace, anyone can change the world.

Every revolution needs an army. That is the real purpose of this book. To use revolutionary language, my objective with this book is to *radicalize* you and get you to become a soldier in this army. Not so that we can destroy some nation, political party, or social movement, but so that we can *collectively use our creativity to attack the world's greatest problems and meet people's most urgent needs*. So that we can reduce the size of the dead-zone at the end of the Mississippi River, like one team has begun to do; or so that we can reduce the size of the carbon footprint of all the computer servers running the Internet, as another team did; or so that we can create the world's least expensive drip irrigation system and help with the global water crisis; or open up the merchant banking systems or literally save tens of thousands of babies' lives, like other teams have done. We need you to add your creativity, enthusiasm, experience, knowledge, and skill to the mix. We need millions of people to join this movement.

So please read on. You can't help but be inspired by the stories you will read. If you do take on the challenge of making, it will change you in exciting and surprising ways—and you might just change the world.

Maker Movement Manifesto

■　■　■

n the spirit of making, I strongly suggest you take this manifesto, make changes to it, and make it your own. That is the point of making.

MAKE

Making is fundamental to what it means to be human. We must make, create, and express ourselves to feel whole. There is something unique about making physical things. Things we make are like little pieces of us and seem to embody portions of our soul.

Make. Just make. This is the key. The world is a better place as a participatory sport. Being creative, the act of creating and making, is actually fundamental to what it means to be human. Secular philosophers like Georg Wilhelm Friedrich Hegel, Carl Jung, and Abraham Maslow all came to the conclusion that creative acts are fundamental. Physical making is more personally fulfilling than virtual making. I think this has to do with its tangibility; you can touch it and sometimes smell and taste it. A great sentence or well-written blog is creative and makes you feel good about what you have accomplished, but it is not the same as the satisfaction that comes from the physical labor involved in making something physical.

If you come from a Judeo-Christian religious background, whether Jewish, Protestant, or Catholic, then you know that the first book of the Torah or Old Testament is the book of Genesis. Read Genesis Chapter 1 closely. Whether you believe in the literal interpretation of Creation or not, we can probably agree on two things coming out of this chapter. God is a maker, and he made us in his image. It is a very powerful introduction to God and who we are as humans. What do you know about humanity by the end of the chapter? It says, "God made" (or "let," or "created") some 15 times and ends with making people in his image. At the end of Genesis 1, we may not know much about God or humans, but we do know one thing for sure: we were made to make.

There is nothing that can replace making—philosophers, religious scholars, and personal experience make that clear. Wars have been fought when the common people thought they were going to lose access to ownership of their own productive tools. So the first thing we must do is make. The do-it-yourself (DIY) home improvement industry in the United States is worth over $700 billion. The hobbyist segment is worth over $25 billion. The most valuable segment of the $700 billion DIY is the perpetual remodeler, specifically those who have enough money to let business professionals do the work for them, but don't. You might know or even be one of these people. In your heart of hearts, you know you don't really *need* to redo the bathroom, or certainly not the way you plan to do it, yourself. But you do it anyway. This is because there is more satisfaction in completing the remodel yourself.

A makerspace is a center or workspace where like-minded people get together to make things. Some makerspace members are designers, writers, practitioners of medicine or law, architects, and other white-collar types who come in and start making things for themselves, their families, and friends. They spend time in makerspaces because they just love to make things. They don't *need* to make Christmas presents; they *want* to.

Tina Albin-Lax had made a New Year's resolution for 2012. She was going to learn how to make something. She signed up for TechShop's basic laser cutter class and has never been the same since. For $60, she learned how to use a laser cutter. Then she booked it for the next day so she could practice what she had just learned, but she needed a project to practice on. As luck would have it, that evening Tina's sibling called and invited her to attend her nephew's birthday party that weekend. With a flash of brilliance, Tina asked for the names of all the children who would be at the party.

The next day Tina used her new training to make cupcake toppers for each of the party attendees. Using the laser cutter, Tina cut out the name of each child and etched in some nice patterns. She finished them with a nice glossy coat and that weekend put one on each child's cupcake. What child doesn't love to see his or her name emblazoned on something? Particularly something chocolaty and sweet? Not surprisingly, the parents wanted cupcake toppers for the rest of their children and then wanted them for their children's parties. It snowballed.

Soon Tina had an online store (www.etsy.com). Then she began teaching classes on how to launch a business and had a great mention in Martha Stewart's magazine, *Martha Stewart Living*. Her phone couldn't make it through the day from all the order notifications she was getting. Last I heard, she was working on a book.

This all came about from a simple desire to make something for the first time since sixth grade. An accidental entrepreneur was born. And what was Tina's background? She was a labor organizer.

I grew up playing neighborhood football with a kid named Ben Parks. His dad was a ceramic artist and had throwing wheels, clay, and amazing glazes around his house. One day his dad invited us all to come out and throw a pot. What a great afternoon. I attempted to make a large vase—and after what seemed like dozens of attempts and lots of help and encouragement—I ended up with a sad-looking, lopsided, very small coin holder. It will hold a couple of dollars' worth of quarters. I glazed it beautifully with help from Ben's dad. A couple of days later, after it had been fired, I got to take it home.

This thing is an ugly duckling that will never grow up, but guess what . . . I still have it. It's small enough that I've taken it everywhere I have moved. Its only value is that I made it and it is some kind of memento from my childhood. Looking back, I realize now that I was not the target of that day of making, though I still appreciate the gift it was. Ben eventually became a ceramic artist himself, following in his father's footsteps. There is something fundamental about making.

SHARE

Sharing what you have made and what you know
about making with others is the method by

which a maker's feeling of wholeness
is achieved. You cannot make and not share.

We make to share. Each of us is wired to show off what we have made. We get a lot of satisfaction out of the making, but the real payoff is in sharing. Some people are coy about showing their work off. Others are just terrified. One of the reasons we may have stopped making is that what we set out to make and what we ended up with may not match very well. Or others may have ridiculed us for our attempts. "I'm not good at making anything," need never be said again. We were born to make. It may take some practice to get good at some kinds of making, but technology has begun to make creating easy enough that everyone can make.

My favorite question to ask at any makerspace is, "What are you making?"

People open up like flowers when asked that question and given any kind of positive encouragement. In this regard, we are all still five years old.

Interestingly, after six years of working in a creative space, I've been told, "I can't tell you everything, but . . ." probably hundreds of times, maybe thousands of times, but I've never been told, "I can't tell you."

Why? We want others to see what we have done.

When I worked at Avery Dennison, we used to let the newest junior product managers help work on the back panels of our product's packaging. They had to work off templates that had been approved and developed for the line, and they had to have all the appropriate approvals; nonetheless, the back panel was "theirs." The young managers would jump into this with gusto, argue over font choices, the kerning of apostrophes, the shade of loam green. I repeat, they cared about the kerning of an apostrophe—the space between a letter and an apostrophe. Look at the space they had to work with here: ' s. Can you see it? On a high-resolution computer screen, this is about the distance of two or three pixels, and they removed one! Yet, they would protect their design turf like a pit bull protects its bowl of food, growling when someone tried to mess with their back panel.

Let me put this into context. To be a junior product manager at any Fortune 500 packaged goods company, you have to graduate from a respected MBA program at the top of your class. You have to work between your bachelor's degree and your MBA at another major company with consumer facing interactions. You are among some of the "best and brightest" our schools and companies produce. You will almost always make senior director, VP, SVP, or CEO if you choose, or you will go out and start your own company. If you are a junior product manager at this level, you are a very intelligent, type A, hard-charging, competitive professional.

That said, once the aforementioned products were launched into the channel and we all went to an Office Depot or Staples to see what the final product packaging and shelf positioning looked like in the stores, the junior product managers would rush like little kids to the stacks of "their" products. They would stand in front of them, momentarily admiring the way the products looked on the shelf and then pull a package off the shelf, turn it over, and examine their handiwork. A sense of satisfaction visibly rolled over them as they saw that the typesetters had taken their ideas into final production and the s was just a little closer to the apostrophe because it had been manually kerned. Invariably, these talented, impressive, type A young professionals would turn and say something like, "I did this."

"I did *this*."

"See the space between the apostrophe and that *s*? I did that."

The glow on their faces was like a new mother's when holding her child for the first time. Complete satisfaction. The need to show others one's new, beautiful child is embedded in the human psyche.

What is going on here? First, while the contributions that these professionals were excited about might seem insignificant—after all, the difference, distance-wise, between the spacing of an apostrophe that has been automatically kerned and one that has been manually kerned is negligible— but the end product is something that can be bought, taken home, and shown to a significant other. Second, it is public. Hundreds of thousands of these packages are shipped all over the world. Third, it is often the first tangible and public representation of years, if not a decade, of work. It isn't the size of the impact that is significant; it is that there was impact and it was made tangible, and tens of thousands of people would "see" their work. That really is powerfully satisfying, even if it is only the amount of nothing between an apostrophe and an *s*.

If you make something and don't share it, was it made? If you make something, even something as small as a one-pixel space modification on the back of a package, and share it, you have made something, and it must be shared.

Another aspect of sharing is sharing knowledge and know-how. The best attribute of a well-run makerspace is the sharing of skills and knowledge. It starts with the formal instruction, but the best learning takes place while one person is building or designing and someone else with just a little (or sometimes a ton) more experience lends a helping hand and the project gets upgraded in the process. The sharing philosophy gives a makerspace its magic. People show off their creations knowing criticism was left at the front door, and everyone feels comfortable asking for help, guidance, and input into projects as they go through the build process. Sharing makes a makerspace a community.

GIVE

There are few things more selfless and satisfying
than giving away something you have made. The act
of making puts a small piece of you into the object.
Giving it to someone else is like giving that person a
small piece of yourself. Such things are often
the most cherished items we possess.

One of the most satisfying aspects of making is giving away what you have made. Wonderfully, most people still value gifts made by the giver more than gifts that were bought off the shelf. If you do nothing else this year, make one Christmas present to give away. And reflect on the level of satisfaction you get and the recipient receives in that act. It is immeasurable.

If your parents are still alive, they probably are still hanging onto craft projects you made for them when you were a child. Quilts are often handed down for generations. A well-made item, meeting a real need, made by and for a loved one, is among the greatest of gifts.

There is another type of giving, that of your creativity or intellectual property. Embrace Global is a wonderful nonprofit that used TechShop for some of its development work. Naganand Murty was one of the design engineers who came to our space, under Embrace cofounder and CEO Jane Chen's direction, to address the problem of infant thermoregulation in developing countries. Babies who are born even a few weeks prematurely are unable to thermo-regulate, or maintain their body temperatures on their own, and consequently must be incubated within one hour of birth or risk death or serious permanent disabilities. For the hundreds of thousands of these babies who are born around the world every year without quick access to incubators (because they are born in rural areas where the nearest hospital with incubator equipment may be several hours, if not days, away), the problem is especially critical.

The question that Naganand Murty and his team had (you'll meet cofounder Jane Chen in Chapter 3) was fairly simple: Would it be possible to design a simple, affordable "blanket" that could maintain a baby's body temperature at a constant level for an extended period of time? And that was not dependent upon a continuous supply of electricity? Well, it turned out the answer was yes. The Embrace portable infant warmer, which looks like a mini sleeping bag and costs a fraction of the price of other baby warming devices, uses some fancy chemistry and design to make it work.

But here is the most amazing thing. Portions of Embrace's core technology were donated to the organization through interactions with other members of the TechShop community. These community members gave their ideas away freely. And as a result, General Electric has signed on to help distribute the blanket, and Embrace is on track to save the lives of 100,000 babies in the next five years. Jane has been recognized by the World Economic Council as one of the top social entrepreneurs in the world.

LEARN

You must learn to make. You must always seek to learn
more about your making. You may become a journeyman
or master artisan, but you will still learn, want to learn,

and push yourself to learn new techniques, materials,
and processes. Building a lifelong learning path
ensures a rich and rewarding making life and,
importantly, enables one to share.

Making brings about a natural interest in learning. It brings out the natural four-year-old in all of us. "Why is the sky blue?" "Where does milk come from?" "How are babies made?" This natural inquisitiveness seems to be beaten out of most people in school or at home. I'll let the educators in this community help figure out why "project"-based learning seems to fit some learning styles better than others, but it certainly feels more natural. I always found the order we did things in physics class backward. Instead of being taught the formula for determining the ratio of the required output force to the input force and then trekking to the lab to see how a lever works, it makes more sense to first observe the lever in action and then learn the formula for it. This is how the principle was figured out in the first place, through observation. You observe an effect, then build a theory to fit the observation. It may be faster to memorize facts than to experience them, but then I would argue you don't really own that fact. "Hot" is a pretty abstract concept until you've burned yourself.

The world is such a fascinating place. How do you design and build a table? What kind of joints can be used to join the legs to the table? Which are the best ones for what I'm trying? What periods in history used different technics? What glues should I use, and when do I use a screw or a nail, or a brad, or a staple, or a rivet? What woods have which characteristics? What style do I want? What tools should I use? The options go on and on. They don't have to; you can jump in and just do it. Or you can plan and plan and plan. The key takeaway, though, is that you are going to learn something. And no one can take it from you.

Learning is fundamental to making. The more time you spend familiarizing yourself with and practicing in a field, the better you will get in it. Very quickly, you will be able to share what you have learned with someone else who is newer to it than you are. There is a different kind of satisfaction that comes from teaching, but it is very real. Watching people you have been teaching become facile and expert in what you have taught them is extremely satisfying.

Learning is fundamental; it is why we have books, libraries, schools, the food channel, the DIY channel, and shows like *How It's Made*. These days, the DIY magazine rack at a local newsstand often constitutes 15 to 20 percent of the total space.

From an educational perspective, we live in a sad time for making. When I was growing up, woodshop and metal shop were required courses for middle schoolers. Every middle school I was aware of had a woodshop instructor. I still have the things I made in middle school woodshop, and many of you do too. Today, it can be hard to find a shop in an entire school district. This makes no sense at all. In our "race to the top," school systems tend to focus only on the students who are headed to college, ignoring the 50 percent of those who aren't, depriving all students of skills that they could use the rest of their lives.

Just as badly, right as we are on the cusp of the largest explosion of new products and development of physical goods through breakthroughs in materials science, 3D printing, bioengineering, nanotechnology, design, and engineering, American institutions are failing to graduate enough engineers, scientists, and production workers. Economically, this is insane. It is time to reengineer our schools and reintroduce shop class. Oh, and by the way, through cheap and powerful design computers and 3D printers, we can make these courses exciting, engaging, and transformative.

With access to the right kind of tools, you can experience your own industrial revolution in a matter of weeks. It's possible. It really happens.

Let me give you an example. A couple of years ago, some of our TechShop staff members encouraged me to meet one of our newer members. He was the first I'd met who was taking an extended "maker vacation." This member had saved up his money for a couple of years working odd jobs as a security guard and janitor, and once he had accrued enough money, he quit his job and took the first vacation he had taken in years.

This man was committed. He had the bug. He wanted to learn how to make things. He was good with the hand tools, but he had never taken welding, machine shop, woodworking, textiles, 3D printing, computer-aided design, or any number of other classes.

To stretch his funds, he didn't stay at a hotel or rent an apartment. Instead, he used couchsurfing.org to find free places to stay every night. A few times, he couldn't find a couch, so he just slept in his car. Couch surfing turned out to be a great tool for him to help us find new members. He was so focused and excited that he would go "home" at night and tell his new couch surfing host all about what he was doing at the shop. We picked up half a dozen or so new members that month. We actually kicked around the idea of turning him into a sales representative by having him couch surf through the Bay Area for a couple of months.

But even better, he became a maker that month. He took every class he could schedule and went from hand tools to power tools to computer-controlled advanced manufacturing tools. He could weld, lay out carbon fiber, CNC mill, lathe a bowl, and spin a lighting fixture. He even picked up a little electronics in that 30 days. His desire to learn was so powerful that he quit his job, stayed at strangers' houses, and created other new makers in his enthusiasm. What is holding you back?

TOOL UP

You must have access to the right tools for the project at hand. Invest in and develop local access to the tools you need to do the making you want to do. The tools of making have never been cheaper, easier to use, or more powerful.

I had to use a phrasal verb as a heading to this section so it would be consistent with all the other one-word headings in the manifesto. I like manifestos heavy with verbs.

You and I are living through the most amazing age in all of human history. Whenever someone asks me which time period I would like to be living in, I always say "right now." Tools are getting easier to use, they are more powerful, and they are cheaper to acquire than at any other time in history. Materials are becoming more accessible, more sophisticated, and more fun to work on and with.

Odds are, you cannot possibly afford all the tools you may want or need. So join a makerspace. What I have learned is that a community of makers does not fully emerge until a complete makerspace is provided. The advantage of a well-equipped makerspace is that it attracts people with a widely diverse selection of projects, creating a beehive of activity, passion, knowledge, and sharing. When a large and diverse set of tools is provided, a large and diverse group of makers comes out to live, work, and play. The following is a general list of what a well-equipped makerspace needs in order to meet the needs of a community. There may be a few more or different tools on your list, but this is a good start:

- Laser cutters
- CNC milling machine(s)
- Manual milling machine(s) with digital readouts
- Manual lathe(s) with digital readouts
- 3D printer(s), consumer and commercial grade
- 3D scanner
- CNC (computer numerical control) waterjet cutter (4 × 8 foot)
- Vacuum forming system
- Heat strip bending system
- Injection molding system
- Commercial grade sewing machines
- Overlock sewing machine (also known as a serger)
- Quilting machine (preferably CNC)
- Computer-controlled vinyl cutter
- Powder coating system (and large oven)
- MIG (metal inert gas) welders
- TIG (tungsten inert gas) welders
- Handheld plasma cutter
- Sheet metal spot welder
- Sheet metal brake (16 gauge × 50 inch)
- Rotary sheet metal punch
- Sheet metal corner notcher
- English wheel and planishing hammer
- Sheet metal shear (6 gauge × 50 inch)
- Sheet metal roller (16 gauge × 50 inch)
- Sandblast cabinet

- Metal grinders and sanders
- Metal chop saw
- Metal horizontal band saw
- Metal vertical band saw
- Electronic testing and soldering equipment
- Large format color printer
- ShopBot CNC wood router saw (4 × 8 foot)
- Panel saw
- Wood planer
- Wood jointer
- Wood band saw
- Wood sanders
- Wood scroll saws
- Wood lathe
- Drill presses
- Granite surface plate with digital height gauges
- Compressed air throughout shop
- Compressed air hand tools
- 30 or more design computers
- 30 or more copies of or licenses for Autodesk Inventor, Maya, 3D Max, 123D Make, AutoCAD software
- 30 or more copies of or licenses for Adobe Illustrator, Photoshop, Acrobat
- 30 or more copies of or licenses for National Instruments LabVIEW Professional development system
- 8 or more National Instruments multifunction data acquisition devices
- Member storage
- Private studios for rent
- Meeting rooms and/or classrooms
- 12 large work tables

- Wi-Fi
- Retail store
- Free coffee and popcorn

And, of course, the local makerspace must then have staff to teach classes and manage this great space.

I'm not going to apologize for the size, breadth, or depth of this list. This is, in fact, what is required to foment a maker revolution. Without the tools and community it is impossible to maintain a movement. Revolutions are fought and won with arms. These tools are our "arms." Without access to them, nothing has changed. They may be easy, cheap, and powerful, but they are useless if *you* can't use them.

PLAY

Be playful with what you are making, and you will be surprised, excited, and proud of what you discover.

The most productive environments I have operated in are often the ones where there is a lot of laughter. We joke about the craziest things. We are playful with the ideas, stretch them to extremes, and morph them ridiculously. Even in the military with the Special Forces unit I was a part of, we were constantly exploring ideas, trying new ways of working, and even goofing around.

One day we learned that the quickest way to cut down a tree was with a detonation cord (det-cord) and plastic explosive. The number of wraps and the amount of plastic varied depending on the size of the tree we were trying to "cut down." The det-cord cut the tree, and the plastic would kick it out in the direction we needed it to fall. If just the det-cord was used, the tree might randomly fall on a nearby object by accident. This became a feature once we figured out how to control the direction of the fall. By using the plastic as well, we could drop the tree on something on purpose. That was a great day, or, it was until we started a small fire. Live and learn. No, actually, play and learn.

We have artists and engineers (among many other categories of users) in our space. What is interesting is that the engineers typically come to a machine with a set of things they are trying to accomplish. The artists, often enough, come to a machine to experiment and see what it can do. (They also tend to break the machines a little more often, and not because they don't know how to operate them; they are just pushing the equipment to do something beyond its normal operating environment.) When the two are combined, watch out. Have you ever heard a CNC milling machine play a tune?

Blocks, LEGO, and Erector sets are what I grew up with. Kids now have LEGO Mindstorms, radio-controlled robots, and Arduino microcontrollers. Soon, the home 3D printer will be the PC accessory of choice. Playing with these toys is a lot of fun and will help to raise up another generation of makers.

Recently, I received a note that one of my sons had updated his Facebook page with a video titled "Hovercraft." I was on the road and had no idea what this referred to, so I clicked through to YouTube and watched him floating around our garage on a homemade hovercraft. He had found instructions on the Internet, gone to the hardware store and bought the pieces he needed, and in an afternoon he had built a poor man's hovercraft using an electric leaf blower as the drive. He now has a hovercraft, and I've got a leaf blower. He was playing around, but he learned how to use a couple of saws he had never used before. I built a trebuchet with my other son and had a blast getting the cats to chase flying paper balls around the house.

Building is a form of play. There are times I have a hard time distinguishing the difference between work and play. I hope you will have the same experience in your work life.

PARTICIPATE

Join the Maker Movement and reach out to those around you who are discovering the joy of making. Hold seminars, parties, events, maker days, fairs, expos, classes, or dinners with and for the other makers in your community.

We are not islands. Though there is a time to work in solitude, to focus, to push oneself without distractions, there is also a time, and I daresay most of the time, where it would be better to be working together, or at least sharing a creative space. The warmth of another human in the room or workspace is preferable to working in solitude. Many artists, engineers, and inventors work alone in their labs and studios, but just as many or more collaborate. Even if they don't collaborate directly, they will seek out the comfort of a peer group to hang out with. Writers form writing clubs, others form co-ops to share tools or workspace. Many go into business with friends or collaborators, not just because they need to, but because they want to. We are social creatures. It is great to be able to build up your shop in the garage or barn, but it is sad to work in it alone day in and day out. It is more fun to work together.

Participation takes many forms: working directly together; attending events; and participating in societies, clubs, and parties with others who care about the work we do and share. One such event, designed specifically for makers by the editors of *Make* magazine, is the Maker Faire. Held in various locations around the world, Maker Faires are annual events where thousands of makers come and hang out together to look at, participate in, and experience a wide range of fun projects that makers are working on in the area. The primary Faire is held in Northern California and attracts over 100,000 attendees over the course of a weekend. Smaller, local versions, called Mini Maker Faires, draw up to a thousand people to see a hundred or so projects, booths, and exhibitions.

The sense of wonder and amazement on the faces of the kids (both young and old) at these events makes all the effort and expense that go into the Faires well worth it. Watching the performance group, ArcAttack, rock onstage inside a Faraday suit while making a 500,000-volt Tesla coil "sing" along with 15-foot-long bolts of electricity striking the suit is unforgettable. Nor will one easily forget the 40-foot-long, fire-breathing, heavy metal–playing metal dragon. Or Colossus, the 70-foot-tall, 25-ton flying boulder merry-go-round where little kids can pull on a rope attached to flying multi-ton boulders hanging over their heads. These engineering entertainment devices thrill and amaze thousands every year. Engaging young people and getting them excited about science, engineering, technology, and math is a key driver of the Maker Movement.

SUPPORT

This is a movement, and it requires support. Emotional, intellectual, financial, political, and institutional support are needed. The best hope for improving the world is us, and we are responsible for making a better future.

Governments have spent billions, if not trillions, of dollars building institutions of learning, research, development, and experimentation. Almost none of them open their labs up to the public. Actually, I'm hedging here, I haven't found any yet that do, but I'm sure there must be one somewhere. We have spent hundreds of billions of dollars on building research institutions across the United States and the world—and within them very little self-directed, self-interested research is taking place. All of that research requires approvals and funding from third parties, a general manager's approval, a budgeting committee's approval, progression through a stage-gated new product process, and the receipt of a grant from a foundation or government.

Instances of access to the tools of research and development outside of institutional direction are exceedingly rare. Why? It is a fact that the tools of the industrial revolution have been exceedingly expensive, hard to use, and of limited power—until now. They are now cheap, easy to use, and powerful, yet we have not made any changes to how we organize access to these tools. This must change. Those countries that change the fastest in this regard will have a serious competitive advantage.

What can you do? Support policy changes at your institution that open up the labs to others in the institution and to those in the local community who don't have access. Help allocate new funding to set up open access fabrication studios. Pressure universities, government research labs, and large manufacturing companies moving into your community to set up open access fabrication studios.

We live in a world now where computers are everywhere. We carry them in our pockets and call them phones. Similarly, the software tools to design and produce things will be coming to your preferred screen; yet without access to a Kinko's for making things (a fabrication studio), you are no better off than before.

Please do what you can to support your local maker community. We have seen a number of technologies come out of makerspaces that have already changed the world. These innovations were created cheaply, quickly, and easily by small teams and, in most instances, by people from outside the domain they were disrupting.

CHANGE

Embrace the change that will naturally occur as you go through your maker journey. Since making is fundamental to what it means to be human, you will become a more complete version of you as you make.

Whenever one joins a movement, one changes. This is a good change. Embrace it. Participating in the Maker Movement is a personal journey. Each will look different. No two makers are exactly the same. No two paths will be the same. But you will change. You will begin to see the world through the eyes of someone who participates in creating. You will look with wonder again at great artisanship. You will wonder how someone was able to design this or that, and you will begin to appreciate local artists, designers, architects, and artisanship in your community. You will wonder where something was produced and who made it—you will look for the story behind the artisanship You will ask about local talent and local sources for things you never dreamed you cared about before.

Joining the Maker Movement and participating in it locally will open up your life to the highest concentration of creative people in your community. You will meet poets, laser etching their words on oak panels, you will meet a financial planner building sets for her children's play. You will see someone start a hobby that leads to an avocation and then a business employing a dozen locals. You will enjoy the excitement and joy of giving those you love a piece of yourself through gifting to them something you made just for them. Join me, join us, join the movement—it will help you become you.

2

Free Innovation!

■ ■ ■

"**M**ark, you need to talk to the guy at the table over there." Every day is an adventure at TechShop. As CEO of the national membership-based do-it-yourself (DIY) workshop and prototyping studio, I love my job and where I do it. Why? Because TechShop is one of the few physical spaces dedicated to fueling the next *economic* boom. And there are a bunch of amazing people, crazy projects, and wonderful things going on here. It is an *Alice in Wonderland*–like place.

My colleague and I wander over to a workstation where a *middle-aged* man is bent over working on a poorly constructed, clunky, aluminum blocklike structure.

"Hi, I'm Mark. What are you making?"

The man, who introduces himself as Mike, grins. "This? This is a desktop diamond manufacturing device."

"A what?"

"A desktop diamond manufacturing device." He chuckles.

"Ask him how it works, Mark," prods my coworker.

Somehow I sense I'm going to be the object of a sophisticated prank. "OK, I'll ask. How does it work, Mike?"

Mike points at the pile of sadly milled aluminum blocks. "First, you need an airtight pressure chamber, like the one I just built. Then you need 95 percent hydrogen and 5 percent methane pumped into the chamber."

Great. Flammable gases under extreme pressure.

"Then you buy a used microwave and scavenge the magnetron out of it."

Like I know what a magnetron is, I mutter to myself. *Maybe it's related to a transmogrifier* (one of Calvin's favorite imaginary devices in the Calvin and Hobbes cartoon series). I decide this person must be crazy—I'm just not sure whether he's crazy in a good way or a dangerous way.

Aloud, I repeat, "The 'magnetron.'"

"Yes, a magnetron," Mike confirms. "You need to get a lot of energy into this thing to create the plasma ball you need."

I need a plasma ball?!

"You can buy special equipment to create the radio waves to get the energy; but that equipment is more expensive than a used microwave, and a magnetron will do the trick."

Hmm, you can get a new microwave for a couple hundred dollars. Do you really need to save a few bucks when you are trying to control a PLASMA BALL in a pressurized cloud of explosive gases?

"So, Mike," I venture. "Hydrogen is fairly flammable. Right?" *I'm thinking Hindenburg.* He nods. "Methane is not inert either . . ." He nods again. ". . . and a 'plasma ball' from a magnetron?" I finish.

"Yep." Mike smiles, pleased that I am following. "And diamonds just fall out."

"Of course." I can't help it; my voice betrays my incredulity and skepticism.

Mike tells me that he plans to fire up this unlikely contraption over the weekend. I confirm that he plans on doing it in *his* garage and not *our* workspace. He points to the holes needed for the gas and the view port from which to watch the diamonds grow (yes, a view port so you can put your face up close to a *plasma ball of energy in a chamber of explosive gas under extreme pressure*) and describes how he milled the thing himself.

I learn that Mike is a physicist who has started two diamond-deposition tool companies over the last 30 years, that he is "crazy" in the good way, and that since the firms he helped to start were focused on tools, they never got into making gems—much to Mike's dismay.

Now he is trying to grow a solid diamond ring for his wife. No metal, just diamond. Singular. He plans to make a large diamond with a hole in it.

What does this have to do with failure-free innovation? Glad you asked. We live in an era now where "nothing" is very close to what it costs to venture. That is one of the major enablers of the coming creativity and innovation explosion: In this day and age, one can "fail for free."[1]

THE $64,000 QUESTION

Edison routinely failed thousands of times before discovering what he needed. James Dyson, creator of the bagless vacuum cleaner, went through 5,127 designs before he was satisfied. Neither viewed each experiment as a failure, but rather as another step on the road to success. This point of view is normal in the product development community. Commercial labs like the one that Edison set up, or that DuPont or 3M run, assume these costs and bear them in development. However, the cost of failure and experimentation drives risk aversion and limits innovation. Which leads me to ask, what is the cost of failure today? What did it used to look like? What other factors limit innovation?

Mike, the diamond maker, is retired. I doubt that he needs to work, but we see him in the shop routinely. Let's "unpack" what is going on from an enablement perspective.

Within a couple of weeks of our meeting, Mike had another pressure chamber milled out and working in his garage. The second version looked much, much better than the "first article." A first article, in new product development speak, is the first physical prototype.

The fully burdened costs (including engineering time, employee time, amortized costs of office equipment, buildings, utilities, shareholder ROI expectations, etc.) of a first article can be extraordinary. Fifteen years ago, you would have needed a $20,000 design computer, $10,000 in design software (or $100,000 if you worked on cars or airplanes), and an experienced mechanical engineer to do the design of a pressure chamber. Odds are, it would have cost $20,000 or more just to do the design. You would have then taken those drawings to a machine shop where they would mill it out for you—another $5,000 to $10,000. And it would not work.

That's the process. It typically takes three iterations, or more, to get to a working first article (assuming you are not doing "new to the world" design work). The time that all this takes, between meetings with the designers, reviewing plans, submitting them to manufacturing, and scheduling all this around other work, is easily six months or more. That just gets you the pressure chamber.

One of the key concepts in design is to fail fast, as time is one of the things that can't be recovered. A classic text on the topic states that half of all the profits of an innovation can be lost with a six-month delay.[2]

Back to our story. I asked Mike what he thought it would have cost to get to his first article if he didn't do it himself. He had been in the business for 30 years and had routinely had this type of work done.

"Eighty thousand dollars," was his reply.

"What has it cost you so far?" I asked.

"Under $1,000."

Would the average reader of this book spend $80,000 to pursue a dream with no assurances that it would work? Probably not. However, my guess is that most could spend $1,000 to pursue their dreams.

The point is this: Failure has now fallen to the discretionary income level. And if it is discretionary, from a macroeconomic perspective, it is free. Amazingly, we have begun to shift nonproductive, *disposable,* discretionary income and time into potentially productive investments while maintaining the same level of spending.

Again, when it costs $100,000 to fail, the money does not come out of our disposable income. It probably comes from a second mortgage if you are an individual. You might be able get it from an angel group or venture capital group, though this is not likely. When something costs that much money, the risks are high and you are using serious capital that has many other potential uses. Conversely, at $1,000, instead of taking it out of the house in the form of a mortgage, borrowing against your 401(k) savings account, or raising it from an angel group, you would likely just use *disposable* money—discretionary money otherwise used on lattes, movies, golf, or a vacation. Money that is "disposable" is generally used to consume, not invest. But now, investments, new product ideas, better mousetraps don't cost $100,000 to develop—they cost $1,000. This allows people to shift their disposable money into development money. The difference here is that development money might provide a return on investment, it might improve the human condition, it might save lives, increase productivity, even save money such that there is more discretionary income. Disposable money used to go to eat does none of this.

The unstated point of "free failure" is that we now innovate for free. A critical by-product of this new reality is that this means almost anyone can afford to innovate. Yes, almost anyone. We just had our first homeless man launch his prototyping service. He had technical skills but lost his place in Middle America due to some medical issues. He found his way back through access to tools.

The "failure is free" idea comes out of the software/e-commerce world. It values the time one spends on a project at zero. It assumes that the computer hardware and software needed are already bought or can be had for free. This is not far from the truth. Today, instead of a $10,000 computer and expensive design software, a $500 laptop and Autodesk Inventor software will suffice to design a first-article pressure chamber.

We often value our time very differently depending on what we are doing and what our opportunity costs are relative to the activity we are participating in. Inventors and innovators see the time they spend creating something either as an investment in the future with hopes of a large return on that investment or simply the cost of pursing their passions. They equate their current investment of time at zero in terms of real current costs. They view the education and training they have received to get them where they are today as a sunk cost (zero). As a result, everything else becomes a variable cost. They have real costs to live and work, but they are doing their inventing in their "spare time." Or they are using their savings or other people's money.

When I ask the entrepreneurs in our space what they would be doing if we were not there for them, most of them say they simply would not be creating a product, tinkering, or working on the next big thing at all. If the cost were going to be $80,000 or $100,000 versus $1,000 and their time, they would just find another job, watch TV, or go play golf.

The choice between innovating or not because of the expense is an "innovation barrier." In the past, the cost to get the information, tools, and resources (money, people, and time) were beyond the reach of all but the most wealthy, passionate, or crazy. At $100,000 invention isn't done. At $1,000 it is! With free software, cheap computers, and cheap prototyping, an invention can be developed. Without it, it's TV time. Welcome to the new world of "free" innovation and creativity.

TARP CLIP

I love 3D printers. They rock. My favorite one prints in three dimensions using plastic wire that it melts and then spits out like an ink-jet printer at 1,400 dpi. It builds the prototype one small globule at a time from the base on up.

A story that the manufacturer of this printer repeats is about a couple of guys who used the 3D printer to create a tarp clip that cinches tightly when a loop of rope is run through it. It speeds up the time needed to attach tarps to the bed of a truck. The inventors used a computer to design the clip. Then they printed out a series of clips on the 3D printer to get the clip the way they wanted it. One of the nice things about this printer is that it produces the prototypes in particularly hard plastic— ABS. This is often a target manufacturing material. Not only did these guys have a "first article," they actually had a production prototype they could show to potential buyers. Very cool.

With the production prototype in hand, these guys created a full-color backing card for a blister pack using a color printer and basic card stock, and they used a plastic vacuum forming machine to create a prototype blister pack. Using these simple tools to create what looked like a finished part, with a professional looking package, in a one-off custom blister pack, the two entrepreneurs took their prototype tarp clip to a large hardware chain. The buyer broke the blister pack open, destroying the only package prototype (to the surprise and moderate consternation of the inventors), examined the clip, and ordered 50,000.

You can do it too. How? Download Autodesk 123D to your computer and get to work. Use a third-party broker to make your production prototype (a few hundred dollars at a place like Ponoko.com or Shapeways.com). Iterate three times in the next couple of weeks. Print your blister pack card on a high-quality color printer at a copy center such as FedEx Kinko's. Use a vacuum former and a vinyl welder to create a package, and start peddling.

For just a few hundred dollars and your time and creativity, you can now create a production prototype that, with a little finishing work, is sales ready. Ten years ago it would have cost tens of thousands of dollars and taken six months to get to the same place. And you still wouldn't have a package.

IT'S THE TOOLS

When Karl Marx wrote about labor and capital, capital (or the tools of production) was much more valuable than labor. Capital was also scarcer. In a mass-customized society with computer-controlled production—or with access to low-cost, short-run tools—we enter a new era in which the tools of production are cheap enough that labor can, for the first time, buy or rent capital as needed. This is revolutionary. It flips Marxism on its head. *Capital* is rented as needed, not labor.

The counterrevolution has begun. Low-cost capital, micro-capital, and free innovation are remaking our world.

OK, so labor can't compete with an oil company, but large segments of the economy are going to continue to give way to the advancement and cost reductions associated with tools, information, and resources.

OUTSOURCE, INSOURCE, AND RESOURCE EVERYTHING

On outsourcing. Some years ago I needed a couple of websites translated into French and German. I reached for my Rolodex (this was more than 10 years ago) and used my old network to find a high-quality firm to do the work. It bid $49,000 with a three-month turnaround, provided we gave it a finished (static) site to code to. I then searched the Internet and used a couple of freelance auction sites to see what I might find for less. I went with a French firm, one of the 90 firms to bid. It had done work for IBM, Microsoft, and a bunch of other large global firms. It translated the site for $3,200 and finished in three weeks while using our live site (which changed daily) as the target. Hello: a greater than 90 percent savings and in one-third of the time.

A friend of mine recently had a custom human resources information system (HRIS) built in India for $12,000. He is reselling it to his clients as a "software as a service" (SaaS) product, in which one rents access to the software on a per-seat basis by the month. He hosts it on Amazon.com's servers, thereby renting computer capacity when he needs it and avoiding the costs of buying, maintaining, and managing servers. In contrast, I spent $60,000 a few years ago just to *implement* an HRIS SaaS solution at a small company, and it didn't work very well. He spent less than 25 percent of what

I did, and he owns the code. No, these will not compete with SAP business management solutions, but a small firm can't afford or manage the big packages anyway.

Today, there are entire enterprise resource planning (ERP) suites being built in the open source community. You can deploy all the software you need to run a decent-sized company without having to pay license fees, and you can rent the servers to run it on. During the dot-com craze, I worked for a firm that spent $30 million on web servers and shut them down well before they were amortized. Today, start-ups rent.

Don't build the back office; outsource it. There are a couple of firms that have sprung up over the last couple of years (Accelcia or Corfino) that will completely operate your financials and back office, accounts payable, accounts receivable, and non-phone-based customer service and become a virtual CFO for you. Some even produce Sarbanes-compliant financials. I use one of these firms instead of a part-time bookkeeper, or a full-time CFO, because they are cheaper, better, and faster.

On insourcing. At another start-up I worked with, we hired programmers across the United States and left them where they were. We saved relocation, office, and computer hardware costs. They provided their own computers, Internet access, and (today) the software would have been free.

I managed my entire team over chat, instant messaging, and cell phones. We had about 12 employees spread across five states. The ones who lived in California I met at Starbucks for their hiring interviews. We hired all but the founders and the CEO over the Internet or at coffee shops. We worked for months without an office. In today's environment, I most likely wouldn't have rented an office at all.

Similar to the days when a journeyman would show up with his own tools in tow, in today's start-up environment, you can expect members of your management team to work virtually out of their homes and provide their own cell phones and computers. The tools just look different. They include a spare bedroom, a coffee shop for meetings, a phone, and a portable computer. This is insourcing. It drives down the cost of innovation. Sure, once you are up and running, the company will take over many of these costs, but the critical phase is at the beginning. Lowering the cost of innovation isn't the only thing; it's everything. Without it, almost nothing happens.

On resourcing. The key thing here is that the costs of resources for a start-up are falling. Cheap computers, outsourced services, outsourced infrastructure, and even outsourced design, production, and manufacturing have never been cheaper.

As confirmation, you might expect to see the development of microventure capital firms or the emergence of a new type of professional, angel, incubator service. Well, you would be right. There are incubator services today that will start you on your Web 2.0 or Internet company (where these trends are the most pronounced) by taking a small piece of ownership in your company and giving you $25,000 to $100,000 to get started. Most of the companies fail (fail fast), but the ones that have worked have worked well. These new companies have a low cost to start up and an explosive growth path.

FAIL FAST

"Patrick," I asked, "How would you describe yourself?"

"Hmm," Patrick responded. "A failed entrepreneur."

"How so?" I wanted to know more.

Patrick explained that in early 2010 he was on his fourth start-up of the year. What he didn't tell me was that he had tried something like six ideas the year before—I got that information from one of his friends. I had gotten to know Pat over the previous couple of weeks because he was taking up more and more time on one of our CNC woodworking machines called a ShopBot (great company, great machine, by the way). We had come to an agreement to help him build 1,000 units in our off hours and help him with the next 1,000 units before graduating him to a local prototype shop that could handle his volume. In other words, he had gone through 10 start-ups in the last year and a half. Wow. That's nine failures and one emerging success. By weighted average, he was right.

Patrick had come to TechShop six weeks earlier and asked one of our Dream Consultants (DCs) what classes he needed to take to learn how to use the tools he needed to create a bamboo-based, book-bound iPad case. This was just before the iPad came out. He proceeded to take the few classes he needed, started to learn the basics of the design software, and leveraged our community and staff to get the design just right. He then produced a few dozen prototypes, created a website, and just before the iPad went on sale, he hired some people through a web-based freelance workplace to distribute flyers to all the Apple fans waiting in line at Apple stores in the major cities. His first sales started to come in through this great little guerilla campaign. Even better, a couple of blog writers were in those lines. After one of them got a bamboo iPad case, he described it as the Rolls-Royce of iPad cases.

Within the next 24 hours, Patrick's team was inundated with 1,000 orders. At $60 apiece and with the other orders having already been received, the team was sitting on $80,000-plus worth of orders. Not bad for a couple of months' work.

About that time, I got to know Patrick. We try to help small entrepreneurs with prototypes and short runs—but 1,000 units of a large case is really pushing the limits of short runs.

Then The Unofficial Apple Weblog (TUAW.com) ran an article on its home page about Patrick's case. You have to remember that back when the iPad first came out there was a lot of hype. If you wanted one, you really needed to get in line at Apple and spend the night or at least a good couple of hours waiting in line. The only people who had iPads in the first few weeks were Apple fanboys (and girls).

These fanboys start their day on two websites: Apple's and TUAW's. You get only official news and updates on the Apple website, so most of them actually start the day at TUAW. And Patrick's iPad case, the DODOcase, was featured as one of the best made. Thousands of orders poured in.

That's about the time that I asked Patrick how he would describe himself. He was standing by the ShopBot supervising another 16 pieces being milled out. Given that this was his tenth or eleventh company or product idea in the previous couple of years, I think, in retrospect, he was being pretty fair. But he had a tiger by the tail.

DODOcase received $1 million in orders in its first 90 days. It did about $3 million that year and was on a $10 million run rate in the second year. I have no idea how it did in the third year, but it had hired 40 employees, saved a bookbindery in the San Francisco area, and started to show up in high-end retailers like Nordstrom. Amazingly, it also counted the president of the United States, Barack Obama, as a customer. Not bad for a "failed" entrepreneur.

A local venture capitalist once asked me how failed entrepreneurial projects impact us. In the venture capitalists' world, most projects "fail," and the company, its staff, and its founders all go away. Somehow he thought we would see the same kind of churn that they did. I was pretty put off by the question, so I told him that, unlike the venture capital world, our members didn't fail. At least not in the same catastrophic way. And frankly, by his definition, they don't. Our members are figuring out what works for their product, themselves, and their lives. When you only spend a few hundred dollars to "fail," it's really just a cheap education and a step toward success. Do that a dozen times, and you will likely move out of education mode into that of owning a company.

When one spends $100 million on some wild venture capital deal and it doesn't work, that is a spectacular failure that the venture capitalist (VC) has to write off. The founders of that spectacular failure, however, may just consider it an expensive education paid for by a venture capital firm. In our environment, rapid iteration (failure) is merely a means to an end, not an end in itself. If the VCs actually invested in founders rather than the firms the founders were starting, and then let the founders iterate a few times on wildly different ideas, neither the VCs nor the founders would "fail" as much either.

What this means is that the VC has a system where big failures are the norm. "Big" as in $500,000 or more. Most of them will not even talk to you unless they can give you $1 to $5 million. So I don't see failure as needing to be the norm; I see learning as the norm. And when "failure" only costs a few hundred or a few thousand dollars, it isn't really failure, it is learning cheaply.

FREE INNOVATION

Tim Jahnigen was one of the first entrepreneurs I met at TechShop. He was mostly working on this weird infrared pet-warming device consisting of two big panels with coils to produce infrared heat rays to warm an animal as it came out of surgery. He told me how veterinarians used wet blankets heated up in a microwave to help warm animals coming out of surgery. And he described how sometimes the blankets were too hot and burned the pet, or how, if an attendant got distracted, all the heat would dissipate from the towel and actually start to cool the pet.

Tim was sure that infrared panels with a timer could do a much better job. He said that he had come up with this idea a few years earlier and had gone to a design and prototype shop to get a bid. The firm wanted $100,000 to do the development and prototype. He didn't have that kind of money to spend on a prototype, so he came to TechShop.

I asked Tim about his background.

"I'm in the music industry," he said. "I'm a roadie for Sting, and I produce shows and write music for other musicians." I was stunned. A self-professed professional roadie working on a medical device?

"What is it going to cost you to get to a functional prototype?" I asked.

"Actually, I'm in short-run production now," he replied. "And it only cost me three grand to get started. I can afford three grand," he added.

From a macroeconomic perspective what just happened here is this: Tim, the roadie, was able to use his personal "disposable income" to innovate a new medical device category. At $100,000, he would have needed investment income, angel funds, VC funds, bank loans, or other forms of capital. But what he did was shift some of his spending, likely from going to see a concert or taking an international flight to catch a rock band performance, and used it to innovate instead.

If one uses disposable income to innovate, there is *no* economic cost. No investment committee, no stage-gated innovation process, no business plan competition, no incubator review committee, no venture capitalist, PE firm, or SBA loan committee. It's just a personal decision to buy some materials, learn how to make something, and then spend the time building it. From an economic perspective, this innovation is free. What was originally going to be leisure spending has turned into innovation spending.

Tim succeeded. The National Institutes of Health (NIH) uses his animal-warming device, and it is in use around the world. Tim the roadie became a successful healthcare entrepreneur—and then he tackled world peace.

Really.

I didn't know it when I talked to Tim that day, but he was also trying to figure out how to make an indestructible soccer ball. On one of his music tours he had seen children using trash for a soccer ball. When he asked them why they didn't have a real ball, they told him that the balls fall apart quickly and there are no replacements.

His next idea was that soccer, a global game, could be used in conflict areas to assist in getting children in conflict zones to play together across political, social, and ethnic divides. Doing so could potentially plant the seeds for peace across a new generation.

After he had had some success with the infrared pet warming device, Tim found a material that would do the trick for the soccer ball project. The ball is made with a new foam material like the stuff used to make Crocs shoes. But Tim thought he would need $300,000 to develop the product. It turned out he only needed $30,000. He described his dilemma to Sting (yes, the musician) over breakfast one day, and Sting agreed to fund the research. Sting's disposable income is a little larger than most people's.

One World Futbol Project is now on track to distribute 1.5 million soccer balls around the globe with the help of Chevrolet and others.

IMPLICATIONS

The information, tools, and resources needed to innovate have never been cheaper or easier to access. When the cost to innovate goes from being a luxury or something that only "capitalists" and venture capital firms can afford to an opportunity that is well within the disposable income of the middle class, then we should expect to see an eruption of innovative products and services as never seen before. When we move people out of retirement and into innovation experiments because it is more fun or maybe even cheaper than a golf habit, or we leverage people's "spare time," they advance the science of diamond deposition.

When we have spaces that allow people to explore a dozen ideas in months for a few thousand dollars, they eventually find an idea worth millions and then create and save jobs.

Or we provide the platform needed for musicians to explore their inner maker instincts to create medical devices or develop products and concepts that improve the lives of the least fortunate among us—and do it with "disposable" income.

I love that word, *disposable*. My thesaurus describes it as "throwaway." Throwaway income. Frappuccino income, golf, travel, cruise ship money. A little money, time, effort, trial, failure, and then success that changes the world is now within the reach of the middle class.

These truly are exciting times, and the gale force winds of "creative destruction" have begun to blow more strongly than even Joseph Schumpeter, who coined that phrase, ever imagined.

3

Communities of Practice

■　■　■

Naganand Murty was sitting at one of our tables in Menlo
Park working on a phase-changing polymer technology.
As part of a class at Stanford's d.school (Hasso Plattner
Institute of Design), Naganand, Jane Chen, and their team had
identified a problem they thought they could tackle. Millions
of children die each year in the developing world because they
are born too early and don't have access to a life-saving incubator. One of the reasons is that incubators cost upwards of
$20,000, even in the developing world. Another reason is that
many villages are simply too far away from a hospital.

Through his engineering training, Naganand knew that
there were materials that could be designed to retain heat for a
long time, could be designed such that they would tend toward
staying within a particular temperature range, and could be
developed cheaply.

As part of the d.school, he had access to sewing machines, but the team was up against some deadlines and needed more than what was available at the school. So he joined TechShop.

Here was a person trying to save babies in the third world. Our community was pretty interested in what he was doing. And that is where the power of the community comes in. At some point in the development of the infant warmer, a polymer chemist with years of experience introduced himself to Naganand and over a short time helped him to redevelop the core chemistry to extend its use.

The largest untapped resource on the planet is the spare time, creativity, and disposable income of the "creative class." As enumerated in Richard Florida's instant classic *The Rise of the Creative Class*, there are 40 million Americans in the creative class. They represent 50 percent of those employed and control $474 billion in disposable income (in 2010). This "class" is an amalgamation of engineers, artists, lawyers, programmers, designers, and others who have the educational or professional propensity to "create." They tend to congregate in "creative cities" that Dr. Florida has rank ordered. This has created a nice consulting practice around helping municipalities do a better job in developing programs and incentives to retain and attract this group of people. The cities at the top of the list are fairly obvious: San Francisco, Austin, and Boston.

The key questions with regard to this group within the context of this book are these: What is the creative class doing to help drive the coming innovation boom? What are the current patterns of interaction we are seeing? And, most important, how can we support and encourage the development of robust creative networks and systems?

First, their day jobs, if they still have them, are likely to be creative by their definition. They may not be focused on breakthroughs, but this group is focused on pushing current products and services, refining them, positioning them, and delivering them. These people are on the front lines of the economy, working to make life happen. Many are focused on making it better, faster, and cheaper. That is what work is about. In a competitive economy, few get to rest on last year's accomplishments for long. They may be attorneys, analysts, or, more obviously, artists and engineers, but the nature of their training and roles in the economy is about creating something, whether it is a great legal brief, fabulous advertising copy, or the left-turn blinker on next year's pickup truck. I'm particularly interested in their "spare time," whether it's actually spare time or, having been recently laid off, between-jobs "spare time."

SPARE TIME

I recently gave a tour of one of our spaces. In addition to seeing the tools, my guest wanted to meet a few of the members. So we got to do one of my favorite things, namely, wander around the shop asking people what they are making. Stopping at a worktable, we spoke with a thirty-something young woman who was working with felt and what turned out to be a laser jig.

"What are you making?" I asked.

"Oh," she replied, "These are high-end, designer iPhone covers for my female friends."

"Really?"

"Yeah, I don't like the covers I find at the stores. They're too masculine, made of plastic, and too sterile for my tastes. So I've found this beautiful red and black felt made with organic dyes that I'm cutting on the laser cutter and then embellishing with various designs. My girlfriends love them; I've started to sell them at some nice boutiques in San Francisco."

"They're gorgeous. What's your background? Have you ever done this before?" I asked.

"Thank you," she said. "I'm working on a jig to try to make it easier and faster to make them. And no, I've never done anything like this before. I was recently laid off from an analysis job where I studied and reported on commercial real estate for a large independent rating agency. I have two master's degrees in business and government but haven't been able to find a job." She smiled, adding, "I've taken a couple of laser cutter classes, become a member, and have started to sell iPhone covers as a way to make some money on the side."

We wished her luck with the iPhone covers and moved on.

I then talked to my guest about the Creative Class as we walked to the back of the shop where a young man was running the ShopBot, a CNC woodworking machine. This machine can cut extremely elaborate patterns into four- by eight-foot sheets of wood up to five inches thick, and it's attached to a computer where one creates the elaborate designs. You see them primarily in high-end cabinet shops.

"Hi, do you mind if we ask what you are making?"

He was working with a very large sheet of stunningly beautiful Plyboo that was lying on the bed of the machine. Plyboo is a green-friendly material made out of bamboo, a rapid-growth hardwood that is more sustainable and "greener" than many woods. It is also beautiful.

"Sure. I'm making Plyboo boxes," the young man replied. "You can see my design here." He pulled up a 3D model on the computer that was controlling the cutting.

"Very nice," I said. "You're making a lot of them." Around 30 box tops were being cut out by the machine as we were watching.

"Yes, I'm working on a 1,000 unit lot right now."

"1,000?" my guest asked.

"Yes. I lost my job a couple of months ago as a lighting engineer, so while I'm looking for a new job, I decided to take a couple of classes and learn how to use this machine. I designed these boxes and sold my first batch to a chain. They liked them and ordered 1,000 at 16 bucks each."

Here was a random sampling of TechShop members, both of whom were unemployed creative class members launching their own jobs. Both of them had leveraged their familiarity with computer tools to expand their experience base and, by using the power of computer-controlled machines to perfectly replicate their designs, had begun to supplement or replace their previous job income.

Another one of my favorite stories is that of Karen Styles, owner of Karetsticks.com. When Karen's husband retired, Karen wanted to be able to work from home rather than be away from the house 40 hours a week. An avid knitter, she decided that what the world needed was bamboo needle gauges.

Pause for a moment. Chris Anderson, *Wired* magazine's former chief editor, wrote *The Long Tail*, where he describes the emergence of small, niche markets that are being enabled by the Internet, search engines, and eBay-like retailers. This is important to think about when you read stories like Karen's.

Karen believed that if she could make these bamboo needle gauges, she could sell them on the Internet. So she started to look into how to make short runs of them. She looked at woodworking tools, outsourcing, and other options and came up blank. She discovered laser cutters and felt that they were the perfect tool for making the needle gauges, as she could cut and etch them in one pass. She could design them in a simple graphics program and finish them with simple tole-painted designs and varnish. Perfect—except the laser cutter cost $25,000.

Karen put her dream of working from home on the shelf for a few months. Eventually, she found us, a place where she could access the laser cutter for a $100-a-month membership fee. She joined, took a few classes, and launched her part-time business. Within months, she was driving across the Bay two or three times a week to try to keep up with all her orders. Within the year, she had quit her job as a program analyst at a major software company, bought her own laser cutter, and was working a thriving U.S.-based manufacturing business out of her garage. Karen launched her new business in her spare time. She used her disposable income to create a new market for a new product. She did it by leveraging her computer skills, a couple of new classes, and computer-controlled manufacturing machines. Her investment to get started was a few hundred dollars.

THE NEW OFFICE

Coworking spaces are the new office, the new community. The best place to work these days is not at work. It's not at home, either. There has been an explosion in telecommuting over the last few decades, and its benefits and pitfalls are well documented. One of the features of the home office is its isolation. It can be incredibly productive. It can also be stifling.

The new arrangement combines the best of both worlds. A coworking space ranges from 1,500 square feet to 25,000 square feet of an open floor plan with desks, tables, and chairs spread throughout the space. Typically, there are quiet areas (no phone calls and limited, hushed conversations), phone booths, and more collaborative areas. Often a start-up can rent a "full office" with a shared printer, secretarial support, mailbox privileges, and the ability to schedule the conference room. There are lots of whiteboards, community events, evening wine and cheese or pizza and beer parties, wireless Internet, and a thriving and intellectually curious cadre of members. Book signings, art events, and classes are common.

General Assembly out of New York has morphed from a coworking space into a twenty-first–century educational institute and coworking space hybrid. Its classes (including web design, social, mobile, programming, database design, and start-up basics) became so popular that within a couple of years it had to scramble to find more space. Venture capital showed up, and General Assembly is now spawning locations across the United States.

One of my favorite coworking spaces—because it is also part of the 5M Project with TechShop (more on 5M later)—is The HUB, a social entrepreneurial coworking space. It is part of the larger network of The HUB Global, with thirty-some locations and growing around the world. You must apply to join and must be working on some kind of project that is making the world a better place. It doesn't matter whether the project is for profit, nonprofit, governmental, nongovernmental (NGO), or personal. As result of this filter—though The HUB attracts some of the most thoughtful, energetic, and interesting people who need not just space and a desk, but ideas, collaborators, and a social network—The HUB is one of the major nodes in the social impact ecosystem globally.

The HUB has hundreds of members at its San Francisco location, holds numerous weekly events, and has launched dozens of companies. A number of nonprofits have moved in, and they have successfully created one of the busiest and most exciting coworking spaces in San Francisco. I'm glad The HUB is in the 5M project and is our neighbor.

START-UP ACCELERATORS

Another form of coworking space, one that is focused on the start-up process, is the start-up accelerator. These accelerators bring together all the resources a fledgling start-up needs into one place. They have the physical space like a coworking space, but unlike a coworking space they only accept start-ups. They then provide mentorships, classes, and money to help get the start-up on the path to success. They usually take a small percentage of the company in exchange for the money and other services.

Plug and Play Tech Center is one example of an accelerator that came out of the Silicon Valley and now has half a dozen locations spread around the world. Again, you need to apply to get space at the accelerator, and you can apply with just an idea. The accelerator brings investors into the mix so that a firm that gets in its door also has the potential to tap an angel investment network. The accelerator is focused on early stage start-ups, almost exclusively software based. Other advantages here are that there are service providers within easy reach. Lawyers, marketing, social, HR, and accounting support have been vetted, often provide discounts, and are used to working with start-ups, thus allowing the start-up to focus on its core technology development. Plug and Play Tech Center also offers lots of classes focused on all the issues that start-ups face, from how to fund an angel round to the more esoteric but critical discussions around deal points that founders need to be concerned about like "collars," "ratchets," "409a valuations," and "liquidity preferences."

I like Plug and Play's position in the ecosystem in that it will take in existing start-ups and plug them into its system. Other accelerators only accept the earliest stage and want to be there at the start of the development of the idea. Y-Combinator exemplifies this approach—it is also an accelerator but plays an earlier role. I like its position in the ecosystem because it is something of a boot camp for start-ups. You don't just show up with a team and current funding and ask for space to work out of. Y-Combinator's approach to coworking is to run an entire cohort of start-ups through the entire start-up process at the same time. Twice a year Y-Combinator holds a competition to see who can get in. It has hundreds of applicants, invites many of the start-ups to pitch days, and then selects upwards of 80 of the applicants to receive a very small seed round of funding, around $20,000 for 6 percent of their company. Y-Combinator then runs these start-ups through an intense training, mentoring, preparation, and pitch practice process that leads up to a demo day. Y-Combinator pitch days now attract top angel and venture capitalists from the Bay Area and around the world.

Start-ups like Dropbox, Reddit, and Airbnb have launched out of Y-Combinator, which has been so successful with this process that SV Angel now guarantees a follow-on investment of $150,000 in the form of convertible debt (with very founder-friendly terms).

The problem with most of these accelerators, in my humble opinion, is that they focus almost exclusively on software. They do this by design, hoping to get enough advertising dollars through capturing eyeballs or traction in a space to force someone to buy the start-up. Or, if the start-up is lucky enough, to keep getting funding through the traditional venture capital route. When you hear about "lean start-ups," people are almost exclusively talking about web, mobile, social network, or apps.

There are some interesting exceptions that incorporate the physical with a software layer. We are seeing this particularly in the "sharing economy" context—companies like

Uber, Airbnb, and Getaround. They are software companies, but they are marrying a physical delivery platform. They are also leveraging underutilized assets, aggregating them, and exposing them through a software delivery tool.

Uber is an on-demand black car service. You download a simple application onto your smartphone, and when you tap the "get a car" icon, you can get a black car to show up wherever you are in the city within minutes. Uber taps into the reality that most black car drivers often have to wait for hours between rides, idly waiting for a dispatcher to call with a new ride. The excess capacity of black cars in a city like San Francisco, New York, or DC is staggering. Yet there has been no easy way to tap into that excess capacity until now. Historically, one would have to call hours, if not days, before a car was needed in order to schedule a ride and then be sure to be ready for pickup when the car arrived. It was very regimented. Uber has enabled me to pack in more meetings in a day in New York and San Francisco just because I know I can get a car through its smartphone application within minutes of asking for one. Uber has bridged the physical with the virtual.

Airbnb does the same thing with house, apartment, and room rentals in thousands of cities around the world, exposing an enormous capacity of rooms that could never have been discovered without this type of service. Airbnb is a website that has aggregated thousands of spare rooms, apartments, and houses around the world that are available to rent like hotel rooms. Owners of the homes or apartments post the availability, costs, and descriptions with photos of their facilities on Airbnb's website for potential customers to view and then rent. The excess capacity of empty rooms, apartments, and homes is enormous. The difficulty of launching a bed and breakfast is very high. So Airbnb has lowered the barriers both to offering a home or room to rent and to finding a home or room to rent. As I am writing this, our family is headed to Hilo, Hawaii, for vacation at an Airbnb home a block from the beach. We get access to a large two-bedroom apartment for the week, and it costs a fraction of what something that large would run at a resort.

Getaround is a car sharing service that lets people use someone else's car. It's like a rental car service, but you rent the car from your neighbor. Again, it has joined the virtual with the physical. Getaround puts a device on the car that allows authorized renters to drive the car. An authorized renter uses a website or smartphone application to find a car she wants somewhere close by and then is enabled through the device in the car to unlock the car and start it. And again, the excess capacity of parked cars in a city is staggering.

An accelerator representative that I spoke with recently told me that upwards of 30 to 40 percent of the ideas that were being submitted for entry into the program were physical, but because the accelerator couldn't support the development of the physical projects, only 10 to 15 percent of the funding was going to these types of start-ups. This means that at an absolute minimum half of the potentially viable hardware start-ups were being turned down because there was no current infrastructure to support them. This clearly needs to be fixed. I am beginning to see progress on the hardware side. First, there are some new government labs focused on clean tech, solar, biotech, and nanotech. In the United States, we also have many university-sponsored accelerators that focus on similar areas. And we have just begun to see a couple of hardware accelerators that are focused more on innovation than invention. In San Francisco, Lemnos Labs started up to replicate the Y-Combinator model with hardware. Members receive access to Lemnos's office, $50,000 in funding, mentorship, and the other services expected at an accelerator. Interestingly, the accelerator didn't buy any equipment because it chose to locate within a few blocks of TechShop. So the start-ups get access to TechShop, too.

The first of Lemnos Labs' successful launches was Local Motion, a start-up that has developed a GPS-enabled device that an organization can put on a fleet of cars, golf carts, or even bicycles and turn them into a shareable platform. Because Lemnos Labs is close to TechShop, Local Motion was able to develop the hardware nearby. It started out in Lemnos' space and then moved production into TechShop San Francisco. One of its first prototype locations was the Google campus in Mountain View, California, where it has 150 electric vehicles and 2,000 bicycles. Local Motion raised a seed round of $1 million from Tim Draper of Draper Associates, Jerry Yang, cofounder and former CEO of Yahoo!, and Tony Hsieh of Zappos fame. Without access to a makerspace, there would be no way to cost effectively run a Lemnos Labs. With access to a makerspace, not only can Lemnos Labs exist, but all the other accelerators in the area can start to pursue hardware start-ups as well. The entire ecosystem becomes more efficient and broader in scope. It isn't just about eyeballs anymore.

CREATIVE CLUSTERS

One of the most exciting collaborations TechShop has been involved in is as a part of the Fifth and Mission project, or the 5M Project, in San Francisco. Forest City Ratner, a large real estate development company, along with the Hearst Corporation, the media company that also has a large real estate presence in California, has been pursuing the purposeful development of a creative cluster in downtown San Francisco. A brilliant vice president at Forest City, Alexa Arena, is combining the ideas and work of Michael Porter, Harvard professor and founder of Monitor Consulting, on regional competitiveness and Richard Florida's work on the creative class.

Situated on four acres in the South of Market Area (SOMA) in San Francisco was a grouping of underutilized buildings owned by Hearst Corporation. Over the years, different portions of the Hearst operation in San Francisco had moved out of the city, were outsourced, or in some instances, closed down due to structural changes to the newspaper business in the last few decades. Hearst wanted to do something special with the excess space, so it partnered with Forest City to see if Forest City could reimagine four acres of downtown San Francisco and make the ensuing development great.

This part of San Francisco sits about one block from one of the worst neighborhoods in the city, Sixth Street. It is also close to rapid transit, great shopping, and the convention center. It is just on the "wrong side" of Fifth Street.

Ms. Arena, using product development and design thinking methods like those used by IDEO, Frog Design, and other top design firms, began a research project to determine how to attract a key group of anchor tenants that would help kick-start a creative cluster. As part of the project, she interviewed a number of start-up CEOs in the city, including Twitter's Jack Dorsey. He was just getting started with his new company, Square, and suggested she contact TechShop because it created its own community. She also pulled in Intersection of the Arts and The HUB, the social cause coworking space mentioned earlier in this chapter. There were plenty of others in the mix as well, but this became the core group that moved into the old Hearst campus at Fifth and Mission. Prior to the project, only Square and TechShop knew one another. Each has a community focus and its own focus and agenda, but each tends to attract members who are creative, artistic, driven, articulate, social, and outgoing.

Each organization had to take big risks to open in San Francisco. Intersection for the Arts, the oldest interdisciplinary art-granting institution in San Francisco, had to "abandon" a part of the city where it had been embedded for 40-plus years. The HUB had a small location in Berkeley, but it had to sign up for three times the space in San Francisco. For TechShop, this would become our first corporate-owned expansion site—and we had to raise $2.5 million to make it work. But each organization did it. Forest City and Hearst helped greatly. Square also committed to the location. Then magic happened.

A digital film school decided it "had" to be close by. Other start-ups decided they, too, wanted to be close. Intersection for the Arts stepped up to take over a gallery space on site. The HUB grew so quickly and started spawning start-ups so fast that it doubled the space it had committed to. TechShop took on another building to handle needs from start-ups that wanted more space. The Monarch bar opened right on Sixth Street. On Wednesdays and Fridays, 5M blocks off a street where Off the Grid, a local mobile food truck cooperative, pulls in half a dozen taco trucks, Intersection for the Arts hosts artists and musicians, and the community shows up for lunch.

About the same time the 5M Project opened, a new organization, SFMade, launched. The brainchild of Mark Dwight (founder of Rickshaw Bagworks) and Kate Sofis (managing director of SFMade), it is a nonprofit organization designed to help manufacturing companies within the city limits of San Francisco. The idea was to become a place where manufacturers could work together on their issues with the city and talk about hiring, manufacturing, exporting, and all the other issues manufacturers face in urban locations. SFMade started by simply locating its "office" on an open table upstairs at TechShop San Francisco. Since that simple, inauspicious start, it has grown to over 350 members and has direct contacts into the mayor's office and local congressional offices. SFMade holds weekly seminars on different topics manufacturers care about and has even expanded outside of San Francisco.

Because of its success, SFMade has begun to help other large cities develop their own versions of SFMade. The timing is right. Manufacturing is coming back, and urban centers have a place in the ecosystem. But getting manufacturing to come back only works if cities understand the unique needs of a manufacturer and work with manufacturers to make them welcome.

The 5M Project is one of the most ambitious of these types of projects, but there are other successful start-up ecosystems. Tim Rowe is the founder and CEO of the Cambridge Innovation Center in Kendall Square, an area of Cambridge near the Massachusetts Institute of Technology. Tim has seen hundreds of start-ups come through in the last decade, and the space the center works within has grown to over 100,000 square feet. The Cambridge Innovation Center's member companies have raised over $150 million in capital and now even have a $45 million start-up fund housed on-site.

I like what Wayne State University has done in Detroit with TechTown along with Dan Gilbert's (Quicken Loans) BizDom. TechTown recently disclosed that it houses over 230 companies, up from 40 just a few years ago. These focused concentrations of tech transfer, accelerators, and seed stage funding can work, though not easily.

PROTOTANK

Adam Ellsworth and Bryan Duxbury decided that they wanted to make a lamp like the one in the Super Mario games. A yellow translucent box with an eight-bit question mark on each side, the lamp is turned on by hitting the bottom, and the user is rewarded with a little sound, just like in the game. Adam and Bryan thought it would be a fun project to build. They had no idea where it would take them. It was simply a personal project.

They leveraged TechShop to create the lamp pieces, using the laser cutters to cut out the acrylic and the silkscreen station to do the basic screen printing. They learned how to use an Arduino board—a single-board microcontroller—to control a simple LED and hacked together a sensor to the Arduino board that detected when the lamp was hit. They were pleased with the result and hung it up at TechShop for other geeks to enjoy their little hack. And then . . .

A gaming blog writer came through the shop, took pictures of the lamp, and posted them online, at which point people started asking where they could get one just like it. Within a few weeks, demand for the lamp grew to the point that Adam and Bryan decided to do a few short runs, set up an Etsy.com store online, and see if they could license the game icon. They gave their project the name 8 Bit Lit and had a hard time keeping up with demand. This is when I met them, through a woman they had just hired.

This woman, whom I had never met before, had approached me randomly one day and thanked me for helping her get a job.

"What are you talking about?" I asked.

"You are a cofounder of TechShop, right?" she asked.

"Yes," I said.

"Well, I lost my job last week," she said. "I decided to come to TechShop to learn how to do some things with my hands while I was looking for work. I became a member today, signed up for the silkscreen class, and now 8 Bit Lit has hired me to start helping them make lamps as soon as I finish the class. I start my new job, here, tomorrow!"

ACCIDENTAL COMPANY FORMATION

People at 8 Bit Lit struggled to keep up with demand for a number of weeks, switched from Arduino boards to a less expensive custom-imbedded chip set, and had an absolute blast working with all their new friends and coworkers. In fact, they had so much fun that after they caught up orders and slowed down shipping, they decided to form a company, keep the team together, and start doing custom contracting work for others. This is another example of the power of community and ecosystems. The environment they worked in helped them to not only make the project, but turn it into a small run and then a company.

A NEW TYPE OF COMMUNITY

What I've described in this chapter is the emergence of a new kind of community that grows up from a community that has a density of creatives in it. But to grow this community, it needs the infrastructure, design, purpose, support, and even building codes to flourish. Those cities that get this right will develop a vibrant creative cluster, and that cluster will produce culture, music, art, start-ups—and jobs.

4

Knowledge, Learning, Control, and Intelligence

■ ■ ■

"Hi, Mark, I want to introduce myself, I'm David Lang," David introduced himself. We were upstairs in Tech-Shop's San Francisco location.

"Hi, David," I said, extending my hand. "Nice to meet you, too." I looked around. "So, what are making?" My favorite question.

"Well, nothing yet," David replied. "I'm just getting ready to take some classes. I wanted to talk to you to make sure that it would be okay if I wrote about my experience here. You see, I don't know how to make anything, and I want to become a maker. I convinced *Make:* magazine to let me write a column on my experiences while becoming a maker. I'm calling it 'Zero to Maker.' I just need to make sure it's okay with you guys if I document what I'm doing here."

"What a great idea! Of course we'd love to have you document your journey. What's your first class?" I asked.

"One of your Dream Consultants suggested I start with the laser cutter. I'm taking that class tonight."

"Perfect," I said. "We call that our 'gateway drug' because it's powerful, easy to use, and extremely addictive—all the things a pusher needs in a gateway drug to get someone hooked." I paused. "So, what *is* your background?"

"Oh, well, my last job was chartering sailboats. The most complicated thing I've ever created was a really good e-mail."

We both laughed.

"I quit that job, and I'm trying to remake myself as a 'maker,'" David added. "Or at least start the journey while I look for other work."

A couple of months later I read his first columns on the *Make:* blog site. I learned that David had joined with a friend, Eric Stakepole, who had started an OpenROV project. "Open," as in "open source," a strategy where in exchange for publishing all the specifications of a project and creating a license where anyone can use the results, people from all over the world contribute time, energy, insight, and money to develop a project. "ROV," as in "remotely operated vehicle." The purpose of this project: to design a robotic submarine that would make DIY underwater exploration possible for everyone. Wow, I thought, zero to ROV is pretty ambitious.

Ambitious or not, David and Eric are making an ROV company. And David is no longer a maker newbie. In the time since we first met, he has taken over 20 classes and visited our space more than 200 times. The OpenROV Kickstarter campaign raised over $110,000, and David now has two jobs—writing for *Make:* magazine and working at *his* company with Erik—and a book project, *Zero to Maker*, which he also crowdfunded on Kickstarter. (Kickstarter is a "crowdfunding" website where people like David post their project ideas and the "crowd"—often friends, family, and Facebook friends—sponsors the project by pledging money through the site. If enough people pledge enough money, the project gets funded. More on Kickstarter later in the book.)

KNOWLEDGE

The creation, development, and distribution of knowledge are interesting things. Whether you want it, need it, or have it already impacts what you know as possible. But wanting it is key. Creating an engineer or a chemist takes time.

When I say "knowledge," I'm talking about the deep knowledge that comes from both book knowledge and knowledge that comes from experience Often knowledge developed through our experience is what encourages us to go back to the book to figure out what is happening. Here are a couple of examples:

A TechShop staff member recently observed, "You know, until you try to mill stainless steel, you really don't understand how hard it is."

What was interesting about this statement was that the staff member had taken the "strength of materials" class required for a mechanical engineering degree, yet he had not experienced it viscerally.

John Seely Brown, former CTO of Xerox and PARC, Xerox's famed research lab, once came to TechShop and told us that many children learn "through their bellybuttons." I love the description. This staff member had just learned through his bellybutton. Hands-on discovery is an important part of knowledge development and a key creator in sparking a desire to learn.

For example, I wasn't very interested in materials strength until one day in Special Forces field training a demo man demonstrated how to blow a hole through a block wall. I was fascinated.

"How did you know how much to use to blow a hole, but not blow up the entire wall?"

He showed me the formulas he used for walls, reinforced or not, bridges (steel, wood, concrete), and the characteristics of different types of charges and explosives. All of a sudden, I was interested in physics. Who knew?

Likewise, I once asked my high school chemistry teacher what had hooked him on chemistry. His reply? "Sodium."

It turns out that pure sodium burns on contact with water. Back in my teacher's day, sodium was easier to get, so he got some. Then he sprinkled it on his neighbor's yard so that mini-volcanos of fire would erupt when the sprinklers were turned on. (Don't try this at home!) He was hooked for life.

Finally, I was at a high-tech conference years ago populated by senior executives from computer software and hardware companies when the speaker asked everyone who had been "the film projector tech guy in school" to raise their hands. Given that only one or two of those people were needed in each room in sixth grade, but that we would probably over-sample, I figured half of the people in the room would raise their hands. Surprise: Every hand was raised. The same was true for, "Who played extensively with LEGOS?" Some folks raised *both* hands on that one. The play value of LEGOS was so visceral that they wanted to give it an extra vote.

True knowledge is born through experience. You have to physically bore into the details of something to fully understand it. Hands-on discovery and exploration are required to innovate. Mastery is required, time is needed—a class on materials is not enough; you have to spend time experimenting in the lab or in the field. True, deep knowledge is hard won and comes with experience.

INFORMATION

We live in the information age. Google and Wikipedia answer our questions. Khan Academy, Apple U, and, increasingly, major universities put their courses online for anyone to find and use. You can teach yourself just about anything now for the cost of a computer and your time. You might not get a degree or certificate vouching that you know it, but the raw information is there for the taking.

Interesting things happen in a world where information is free, easy to obtain, and ubiquitous. The biggest is *transparency*: Everyone knows how much Best Buy wants for the latest gizmo. It's posted online. You can shop Amazon, Craigslist, Best Buy, and hundreds of other merchants right now from your cell phone. There are no longer sunk costs in driving down to the store or mall to find out what an item is selling for. This is "friction" free information: pricing information is available when you want and need it, and you don't have to pay anything for it. This information falls into the category of "search and find costs." In the past, search and find costs were very high and led to suboptimal purchases— seriously expensive suboptimal purchases.

There are two sides to a sale, though. It isn't just that the consumer is trying to find a store; the store is often trying to find the consumer. So the search and find function works both ways. As you've probably experienced, you can save a lot of money by shopping online and finding the thing you're looking for cheaper from an online store. This is true for a lot of purchases, not just consumer purchases.

During the dot-com craze in 2000, as this friction-free flow of information was just starting make itself felt, I was at a firm that needed an animated logo—a cartoon. So we searched through our Rolodexes for a few design firms we knew that could do this kind of design. We also posted the project on an online job board. Through the traditional methods, we received a number of inquiries and bids in the $20,000 to $40,000 range for the work. But because we had posted the project online, we also received some tremendous bids from lots of smaller players, independent designers, cartoonists, and even a couple of traditional firms. We also, and this is a big "also," got an inquiry from a local artist who had been looking to branch out a little and experiment. He liked the idea of working with a start-up. He agreed to do the job for about $5,000. Not bad, but not cash—he wanted stock. *Great.* Cash-starved start-ups have stock, not cash.

Now, many of you are going to think, and rightly, "So what? You saved some money on the Internet. Big deal." What I failed to mention is that this was an internationally renowned, Pulitzer Prize–winning cartoonist.

So let's review. This result exceeded all possible imagined outcomes—by a very, very big margin. The likelihood of getting a great design had just gone through the roof. The outcome was better. It was faster—the artist lived within five minutes of our office—and it was most certainly cheaper: He did the work for stock. Better, faster, and cheaper than the old-fashioned way. Can you imagine reaching into your contacts manager and pulling up a Pulitzer Prize–winning *anyone*? Then asking that person to do some work for you on the cheap? For stock? And you want him or her to visit your place next week to review the ideas?

This is what friction free means: both buyer and seller get connected more quickly, cheaply, easily, and sometimes with profoundly better outcomes.

The Internet also helps to reduce "sacrifice." This is what a customer has to put up with in order to get his or her needs met. There are no perfect products, and because products have a specific utility designed into them, the designer has to make trade-offs. Alas, the tradeoffs aren't always what the customers like. The item's too big or too small, it's not the "right" shade of red, it doesn't match other accessories, it comes with a limited warranty, or you need more of it than the seller has.

Take, for example, a simple No. 2 pencil. This should be as close to a perfect product as there is. It's ubiquitous, cheap, and it's been around for ages. It's made of simple materials—wood, graphite, glue, and a little metal band holding the eraser. Until I tried to understand the concept of sacrifice, I had never looked at a pencil particularly closely. It's a pencil. But think about it. Do you like the scratching sound it makes when it writes? I don't. Do you like sharpening it? Why do we have to do that? The eraser doesn't actually work very well, and it's not big enough. The graphite breaks too often. The line width is inconsistent as the tip gets dull. The graphite smears and gets on my hands. It's a really yucky yellow. It doesn't taste very good when I chew on it. Hey, I chew on it. It should taste like cherries. It doesn't have a cap for when I put it in my pocket. It isn't very strong. It's either too long or too short; I like mine midsized. I have to throw it away before I use all of it. I have to carry a sharpener. It makes a mess when I sharpen it. I waste graphite when I sharpen it. It's not legally binding when I sign documents with it. It isn't classy. When was the last time you proudly pulled out a yellow no. 2 pencil? It's just a pencil.

How much customer sacrifice do we put up with in other areas? Lots. One of the things that the Internet does is enable producers and consumers to better match with one another. If you think about that for a little bit, you begin to expect to see more producers selling fewer items today than you did before. And you would be right. I was thrilled to run across this gem of research from the Social Science Research Network because it proved that this is in fact what is happening. The Internet has changed the landscape of what is and what can be sold:

> Amazon's Long Tail has gotten significantly longer from 2000 to 2008 and ... overall consumer surplus gains from product variety at Amazon increased five-fold from 2000 to 2008.[1]

The term *long tail* has gained popularity in recent times as describing the retailing strategy of selling a large number of unique items with relatively small quantities sold of each—usually in addition to selling fewer popular items in large quantities. The long tail was popularized by Chris Anderson in an October 2004 *Wired* magazine article in which he mentioned Amazon.com, Apple, and Yahoo! as examples of businesses applying this strategy.[2] Anderson elaborated the concept in his book *The Long Tail: Why the Future of Business Is Selling Less of More*.[3]

And this research was concluded before the most recent economic downturn when people started thinking more about what they bought. When one purchases less, less frequently, and with more purpose, one focuses more on those acquisitions and wants them to be more useful, better constructed, fabricated by local suppliers, with local materials, and to come with a story.

IKEA and furniture chains like Ethan Allen will discover they are dinosaurs in the next decade. Why would I choose furniture that comes in the wrong size, with the wrong finishes and limited choices, isn't customizable, isn't personal, and is constructed by someone I've never met? Particularly if I could download the basic designs, mash them up, make them mine, and have a local artisan produce them for me? IKEA may be able to manufacture it for less than the local artisan, but so what? There is so much customer sacrifice with the retailer's furniture that IKEA doesn't see and isn't positioned to capture, it makes me cringe. And any local artisan can match Ethan Allen's prices and make the furniture locally sourced, potentially from recycled material, and imbued with more meaning because you can get to know the artist, select the wood, and work with the artist on the design. What if *you* made the furniture yourself?

When I got "the" big promotion to senior product manager a couple of decades ago, my wife and I decided it was time to buy some "real" furniture. We purchased a gorgeous set from a high-quality national branded furniture company. We got plenty of furniture for the $12,000 we put on credit (and spent the next four years paying off), and for a solid year I felt good every time I came home and saw those beautiful pieces sitting in our living room. But now I get no psychic boost from the purchase. The furniture is still beautiful, well made, high quality; we are still satisfied with the purchase. But if I were to do it again, instead of buying the living room set, I'd make it myself at our shop with my wife, who has always loved woodworking but could never afford the tools.

True, this would be a serious investment of time. We would have to skip a lot of quality TV time. But we might make a vacation out of the adventure and get the kids involved— to build something together that we would cherish until our dying day and then bequeath with pride to our children. If you don't have the time to make the furniture yourself, you could find a local artisan through the Internet with whom you could collaborate. You would have input into the design of the furniture, and it would still be more meaningful than picking it up at a store.

One of the cool things is that CNC production capabilities will begin to increase an artisan's fabrication capabilities, allowing him or her to more effectively compete with the larger manufacturer by increasing the artist's productivity, and when that happens, everything changes.

Watch for IKEA or Ethan Allen to try to compete with this new ecosystem and to open up a "local" section in their stores and online catalogs. Watch for them to add more customization, local artists, and DIY sections where you can participate in the build or design process. They have to evolve, or, like the dinosaur, they will go extinct.

LEARNING

I've talked about knowledge and information in this chapter. Let's move on to learning. Classes, books, and online instruction accelerate the acquisition of knowledge, and the acquisition of knowledge is one of the many things that is driving the Maker Movement. Why? Because now one can rapidly pick up the knowledge needed to make something. Helping this is the development of software that makes it easier and easier to control machines, so there is less to learn.

The online universe is exploding with instruction. From Khan Academy to Lynda.com and Instructables, it's possible to learn calculus and what the third derivative is, how to code in Java or use Ruby on Rails, how to construct an electric guitar, build your first robot, or thousands of other projects—from the comfort of your own home, on your own schedule, and for a fraction of the cost and time investment of traditional classroom learning.

In the past, if you wanted to personally learn how to make something out of plastic using molding machines, you could choose the trade school and apprentice route, maybe a junior college, or go through a full four-year bachelor's degree in mechanical engineering (and risk not actually getting to use mills and lathes or an injection molder). Both of these could easily take years. Now, you would sign up for a few specific software classes (two or three class sessions), a couple of CNC classes (two or three class sessions) and an injection molding class (one class session). You would then have enough skills to at least get started—this month.

The New York City coworking space General Assembly started out as mostly a coworking space and has morphed into a coworking space with serious educational training opportunities attached. General Assembly teaches user interface design, software programing, and other cutting-edge training that prepares one for a job right now. Classes run in length from one night to eight weeks. General Assembly is about to launch intensive several-week-long training in technical areas for which U.S. universities will not be writing curriculum for years. This is relevant, rapid instruction from real-world practitioners.

At our shop, we impart the minimum amount of information learners need to operate a machine safely and move their projects to the next step. It's a focus on adequacy rather than mastery. We don't offer 12 weeks of instruction on anything. The reason educational and vocational courses are 12 weeks long has more to do with keeping kids off the streets and not competing for work and keeping educational institutions and teachers profitable than it does with content mastery. I love our educational institutions, but they are designed the way they are for many other things than just imparting knowledge at the right time in the shortest period possible.

You want to learn how to weld? You can go to a trade school and then apprentice for months or maybe years, or you can find a local community college that offers a 13-week course on welding basics. Alternatively, you can buy a welder, watch some videos, and fire up the welding equipment in your garage—and risk burning down your house. Or you can find a makerspace and for $60 learn to weld in a couple of hours from an expert.

You won't be a very good welder at the end of our two-hour safety and basic use class, but you'll know the basics of welding and how to operate the equipment safely, and you will weld something. The odds are very high that you will be able to produce useful things with even this little bit of welding experience. And with some practice—well, lots of practice— you can get good at it. Good enough to finish your project without spending 13 weeks in a classroom or spending a few hundred dollars on your own welder and then storing it for the next decade.

What else could you learn in a day? Basic woodworking, how to use a laser cutter or sewing machine, how to use a waterjet cutter to cut four-foot by eight-foot sheets of steel, CAD/CAM basics, concepts of computer numerically controlled (CNC) machines, the basics of 3D printing or vinyl cutting, powder coating, sandblasting, basic carbon fiber, basic electronics, or dozens of other things. Yes, it is possible to go through your own personal maker revolution in the next 12 weeks.

CONTROL

Computer numerically controlled (CNC) milling machines, along with 3D printers and other computer-controlled tools like that laser cutter, plasma cutter, and waterjet have remade manufacturing over the last couple of decades.

Beginning in the early 1950s at MIT with the first development of a computer-tape, automatically driven, numerically controlled mill, there has been a steady rise of the CNC machine. Moore's law has helped to drive down the costs of the machines and totally revolutionized the design profession. The day of the drafting table's demise was predicted as early as the late 1950s and early 1960s. It took a while, but computer design has won out over drafting. With that, the ability to copy, modify, and produce has become much easier.

At first, these machines were extremely expensive and hard to use. A user had to learn an esoteric scripting language called G-code to make anything. With the development of easier-to-use software tools like Autodesk Inventor and even easier-to-use software like Autodesk 123D Make, the universal accessibility of design tools for making things has become a reality. You don't need to program in G-code or even know how to spell it. Some of this software is free. There are also online libraries of files that make parts so you don't have to do much at all to get started.

The ability to design and develop something in 3D on a computer and then use various tools to produce it is stunning. With the development of computer cloud systems that allow users to tap into the power of networked computers on the Internet, the ability to do very powerful development is now at the fingertips of anyone with a computer and access to the Internet.

With more advanced tools like Autodesk Inventor, one can even model simulations, stress analysis, strength, wear, and functionality. Using a design software's materials library and a finite element analysis engine, it is possible to swap out different grades of steel or aluminum on the fly and rerun a 10-year wear simulation in minutes.

What has really changed the "control" aspect of innovation and creation or manufacturing in the last decade is a combination of the price and the increasing capabilities of software and enabling platforms. Until very recently, good computer-aided design software tool cost between $5,000 and $100,000. But not anymore. A TechShop partner, Autodesk, began making "consumer" grade versions of its software available free. This is the same core engine for which the company charges thousands of dollars. Sure, Autodesk has removed items like finite element analysis, but what does the average maker care about that? And if you really do need that, come in and use one of our computers; they have all the fancy, expensive software you need.

Just as wonderfully, free libraries of cool designs are popping up. Autodesk, through a website, is supporting a community of people uploading designs, and other sites support the open hardware movement and provide free designs. Thingiverse.com is great. You can download the files and modify them to meet your particular needs. Type "thingiverse unicorn" into your Internet search engine and go to the thingiverse.com site, and you'll see half a dozen unicorn designs that you can print on a 3D printer or modify and then print.

The three most popular tools at TechShop are the laser cutter, ShopBot CNC wood router, and 3D printer, each of which can be learned in a couple of class sessions. Our members routinely launch new careers after learning how to use the laser cutter or ShopBot, and we save tens of thousands of dollars at each location we build out by using the ShopBot to build furniture for everything from our flat pack front desk to signage and storage bins. (Flat pack is a method of using flat four-foot by eight-foot sheets to build desks, stools, chairs, and tables.)

What has happened over the last couple of decades is that the stepper motors and computer chips that control CNC machines have become so powerful and affordable that they are now being attached to amateur-level machines. The software is getting so easy to use that it's possible to go onto youtube.com or a software company's website and watch an instructional video, or take a simple introductory class, and begin making simple things within a week. This kind of rapid productivity has never before been possible.

In the past, if you wanted a small nightstand with a relief of your children's faces carved into it, you would have had to hire a craftsman to build it for you, or attempt to make one yourself, freehand. Now you can take some digital photos of your kids off your computer, run them through a filter to give them depth, convert them to woodcutting instructions for the ShopBot, and make the nightstand this weekend. At a maker-space, you can accomplish this with three classes to become familiar with the necessary equipment, some free software, and a little experimentation to make something that your children will want to keep for the rest of their lives.

The "control" aspect of this revolution is hard to over-estimate. At the national level, the U.S. government's interest in advanced manufacturing as a competitive opportunity to bring manufacturing back to the United States is being driven by this capability. I'll talk about that more in a coming chapter.

PERSONAL INDUSTRIAL REVOLUTION

The first industrial revolution started around the year 1760 with the invention of mass manufacturing machines. The tailor uprising in France that contributed to the French Revolution was a direct result of the understanding of the tailor guild that its members' way of life—their control of the tools of production—was being taken over by mechanization. As the development of the industrial revolution went forward, opposition to the new realities of production developed, eventually with Marx developing the idea that the tools of production should be owned by the state, not capitalists. I would postulate that few people joined the communist revolutionary movements because they truly believed the state should raise children apart from their parents. People joined the party because they were losing control of their means of production. For thousands of years, people owned their own tools to accomplish their work. They produced with their hands and their tools. With the rise of industrial machines, it became too expensive for individuals to own the means of production, and average craftspeople began to lose control of the tools they used to produce and thus became laborers.

Improvements in driving these machines came through the introduction of the steam engine, the refinement of the steam engine (the by-products of which were water pumping systems that allowed miners to mine more deeply for coal and ore), and the birth of the modern steel movement. Electricity came along, possibly the demarcation for the beginning of the second industrial revolution, bringing with it lightbulbs and electric engines, and over a period 150 years life was truly revolutionized. There is a lot of debate among historians about the timing of the start of the industrial revolution, as well as if and when the second industrial revolution occurred. Prior to electricity, industrialization was driven primarily by steam. The old plants had huge conveyers transferring power around a plant. With the discovery of electricity and the invention of electric motors power was more easily distributed.

Eventually the industrial revolution was exported. Japan went through its industrial revolution much more quickly in the 1870s, followed by the rest of Asia, including India and China a century later. Each time, the cycle shortened until the industrialization of a nation could be accomplished in 10 to 20 years. But still, the tools of industrial revolution were confined to those who could afford them—namely, big businesses.

Then, in the 1960s and 1970s, the Japanese started to produce capital tools and drive down their costs. Right behind them, the Chinese came in and drove down the costs still further. Over the last 20 to 30 years, there has been a greater than 70 percent reduction in the price of just the basic mill and lathe. One can now get a good lathe from China for $5,000 or a mill for $10,000. This is expensive, but not beyond the reach of a small business. As a result, the tool and die industry in the United States has all but dried up with the combination of inexpensive tools and cheap labor from other countries.

In parallel with this trend over the last 20 years, computers have been following the well-known Moore's law wherein computers double their capabilities every 18 months while maintaining their price. Initially, they were very expensive. Attach a computer and software license to a milling machine, and you added $120,000 to its cost. In addition, the operator had to learn how to program G-code and the software that produced it, which typically took six months to a year, assuming one knew how to use a mill to begin with.

All this has changed. Computers have invaded the manufacturing floor. Instead of costing $250,000 to $500,000 for a CNC mill, it's now possible to purchase one for less than $20,000, including the software. This is still a lot of money, but if you use a membership makerspace that has one, you can have access to it for around $125 a month. In addition, the CNC software is getting easier and easier to use; I see people go from introduction to producing useful parts in less than a week. I believe we are on the cusp of a third industrial revolution. Chris Anderson has called this the "New Industrial Revolution." It is being driven by inexpensive access to easy-to-use and powerful computer-controlled tools, including the magical 3D printers. Access to a complete innovation lab like a fully equipped makerspace has dropped by four orders of magnitude. With the development of pay-by-the-month maker-spaces access to these tools are 1/10,000 of what it would have cost just 10 to 15 years.

I started this chapter with David Lang, someone who had never made anything, but who through classes and access acquired enough knowledge and experience to take a leading role in developing a robot company, David essentially went through his own personal industrial revolution in about 90 days. Not 150 years, or 30 or 10. Ninety *days*. Hello. People can now go through their own personal industrial revolution for hundreds of dollars, not millions, and they can do it in weeks, not years or decades. It is not unfair to call it a revolution.

I met Perrin Lam much the same way. He introduced himself to me by saying, "I just want to say thanks for opening here in San Francisco. My name's Perrin, and I'm remaking myself."

Perrin is an older gentleman, a copywriter by profession, with probably close to 40 years of experience. He had started out at a big ad agency decades earlier, worked on big brand, advertising campaigns, and eventually went to the client side. He ultimately ended up writing advertising copy for a major newspaper, where he had good long career until the Internet and Craigslist all but destroyed the newspaper business. That's when I met him, about a week after he lost his job.

"Imagine my dilemma, Mark. I'm a 60-year-old news-paper copywriter. Who is going to hire me?" Not waiting for my reply, he continued, "I'm going to become a jeweler. I think that laser cutter can do just what I want it to."

I recently ran into Perrin, and he was excited. It's been a couple of years now, and he has begun to sell his jewelry to the local museum store market. When I ran into him, he was getting ready to attend the national museum store buyer convention to show off how he could customize jewelry to match the unique character or domain of the museum.

One of the great things about remaking yourself is that you don't forget your other skills. Perrin's website, business cards, and brochures absolutely sing. You see, he is a pretty good copywriter.

INTELLIGENCE

There is a great deal of interest in the concept of advanced manufacturing. This is a large and diverse topic. Most of the press coverage is focused on the 3D printer as it is the "new" thing (as much as a 25-year-old technology can be new), but the field also includes CNC, robotics, and software. Design software tools are getting sophisticated enough now that they will do failure and manufacturing analysis and make suggestions on how to change a design to make it more manufacturing friendly.

A truly intelligent manufacturing system would understand what you were trying to make and would know what manufacturing capabilities you had, the quality you were trying to achieve, the materials at your disposable, the cost constraints you were working with, and a range of other needs. It would then interactively help you to optimize the product you were trying to make within the constraints it was given. It would also provide a complete set of automated (or, more likely, semiautomated) instructions on how to manufacture it in a flexible manufacturing environment. If that environment were a highly automated manufacturing location, one could envision limited human interactions. That's the goal, anyway.

But let's keep going. Many components will come with smart sensors. I worked on a project years ago that envisioned a future in which parts would know how they were doing (if they were broken, cold, stressed, bent, etc.) and could signal when a problem was developing. Imagine a bushing in an automobile with a cheap sensor that, when deformed, would send out a signal that it was about to fail. It isn't hard to imagine, then, a whole series of events being kicked off that would ensure a replacement was made for you, staged, and ready for repair the next time you were at the dealership. Mind you, it isn't broken yet, just getting ready to break. And when the above problem is tied into an advanced, distributed manufacturing system, the part would be made on demand at the time of need. It might not be the exact same part—replacement parts are a big business for automobile companies, and the parts markup is huge. A car company also has to carry the inventory and distribution costs. The automobile company might make more money upgrading the part slightly so that it could be made locally on demand.

I could see internal plastic components being laser sintered out of aluminum as a "cheaper" solution that is actually better from the consumer's perspective. Again, a typical new replacement part is three times as expensive as the original part integrated into the automobile because of all the carrying costs associated with it. Also, you can't always get just the part you need. I replaced an entire handle system on a car recently because a plastic piece broke, and I paid over $300 for the parts and $100 for the labor. Milling the piece out of solid stainless steel might have been cheaper than replacing the entire assembly. In the not-too-distant future, this ability to make parts on demand will become a viable option. And the car companies might actually make more money on it.

To recap, intelligence will not just be part of the advanced manufacturing platform but will become imbedded into the parts, components, assemblies, and systems it produces. This creates an entire ecosystem tied together through robust digitalization, communication, status checks, and work flow. Intelligence indeed.

Fueling Innovation

■ ■ ■

CROWDSOURCING

Ben Young came up to me one afternoon to introduce himself.

"Hi, I'm Ben. I just want to say thank you for building Tech-Shop and helping people like me launch new products."

He and his brother Ivan Wong, along with a friend, Anne Bui, were working together on a project.

"Nice to meet you, Ben. Thank you for being such an enthusiastic member," I replied. "So, what are you making?"

"Well, you see, I'm a professional sports photographer," Ben said. "Do you know what the problem is with professional SLR cameras?" Very animated, Ben clearly believed there was something about a camera that needed to be fixed.

"I have no idea."

"Well, the loop strap mounts on a camera are on the top of the camera body. This is, like, the worst possible place for the strap—okay, it would've been worse if the mounts were on the lens. Anyway, my partners and I have been e-mailing and talking to all the camera makers, trying to get them to put the straps mounts on the bottom of the camera body so that the strap won't be in the way when you are trying to take photos." Ben paused. "I can't believe the camera companies aren't listening to us. But they aren't."

I nodded.

"As a sports photographer, I find the straps are a real problem sometimes; they get in front of the lens and in the photo if I'm trying to move with a fast-moving car or athlete." Ben was on a roll. "And, ergonomically, it would be easier to grab a camera and get it into position if it were upside-down and I could just grab a corner of the camera body, move it to my eye, and shoot. We often carry a couple of cameras at a time so we don't have to change lenses. It's just stupid design." Ben finished with deep disappointment in his voice.

"Wow, I had no idea it was that much of an issue," I said. "So what are you doing about it?"

"Well, we are professional photographers, not mechanical engineers, but we have been able to build a bunch of prototypes after taking some classes and getting some help from our partner, Anne Bui, a product designer for Fox Racing. . . . Because our prototypes don't hold the camera in just one position, but let it swivel on our loop design, it makes it even easier to protect the lens by having it swivel in close to the body and not stick straight out when we aren't using the camera. We call it C-Loop."

"What is the design?" I asked.

"We came up with this." Ben showed me a prototype and proceeded to explain that the C-Loop bolt was designed to thread into the camera tripod-mount hole at the bottom of a camera, with two loopholes for the straps close to the mount hole. The built-in swivel is small, unobtrusive, and solves the problems photographers have with the top-mounted design.

"Nice," I said encouragingly. It looked like something of a niche product, but clearly an upgrade to most strap mounts. "What are you going to do now?"

Ben lit up. "We're going to try Kickstarter and see if we can raise the $15,000 we need to do a production run. We've found a place in San Francisco that can manufacture it for us, but they have minimums, so we need to order 500 at a time."

"Wow, that's great. Locally made, too. Good luck with the Kickstarter campaign."

A couple of months later, I ran into Ben and his brother Ivan.

"Hey, so how's the Kickstarter campaign going?" I asked.

With a great big smile Ben said, "Fabulous! We've raised over $60,000. Anne quit her job, and I'm not going back to school next semester."

"What's next?" I asked

"Well, first we have to deliver on the ones that have been ordered, but we are getting inquiries now from some retailers and distributors, and we're leveraging this to launch a camera accessory company."

KICKSTARTER

Launched in 2009 by Perry Chen, Yancey Strickler, and Charles Adler, Kickstarter is the largest crowdfunding site on the web. Initially focused on all forms of art (including film, theater, journalism, and photography) and then quickly into almost anything imaginable that the folks at Kickstarter thought was cool, Kickstarter, Indiegogo, and other websites like them have become the go-to, web-enabled platforms to get projects and now product ideas funded by the crowd.

The way it works is this: An artist or entrepreneur comes up with sponsorship levels for the project he or she is working on. Say pledging $5 gets you a postcard, $20 gets you a T-shirt, and $35 gets you the item that's being launched. The artist sets a minimum threshold needed to get the project done (which can lead to problems if the amount is set too low) and then goes through an application process. If the application is accepted, the project goes live. In C-Loop's case, Ben and his team were looking for $15,000 and gave themselves 42 days to raise it. By setting a threshold and not funding the project if the threshold is not reached, "investors" or "customers" don't run the risk of being part of a partially funded project that they have put money into.

The founders of Kickstarter wanted to figure out a web-enabled way that their artist friends could point to that would help them raise money. It has become wildly successful. For example, Pebble, a watch idea that uses a wireless interface with smartphones, famously raised over $10 million on Kickstarter after seeking $100,000.

Online crowdsourcing really changes the fundamentals for financing products. It democratizes access to capital in a way we haven't seen since the Glass-Steagall act of 1933 made it illegal to advertise for investors. But this is even better, for the artists are not selling stock, they are preselling products or projects and as such aren't giving up a piece of their companies.

A subtle result is that this platform has become a natural conduit for launching "lifestyle" businesses. A lifestyle business is one that provides an income to the founders but isn't large enough or profitable enough to become a "big" company and have a big "exit."

If you take money from an angel group or venture capitalist, they will want to see a big exit (lots of money coming back). They don't fund lifestyle businesses. Family, friends, and the bank have historically been the only sources of capital, outside of savings or credit cards, to launch lifestyle businesses. But friends, family, and banks are often not in a very good place to assess the likelihood of someone having a product that will sell. So this solves both issues: you don't have to be planning on a big exit for professional investors, and you don't have to ask your family or friends to lend you large amounts of money or invest in your business. This platform helps to prove or disprove whether it is a good project or not by whether enough money was raised to fund the project. Brilliant. And better, it funds things that would likely be impossible to get funding for from traditional sources.

Crowdfunding of art projects, services, and products has been so successful that in 2012 Congress revisited the idea of crowdfunding and passed the JOBS (Jumpstart Our Business Startups) Act, which will allow companies to sell securities and raise loans through crowdfunding portals. The JOBS Act promises to jump-start the entry-level economics for start-ups in the United States by making it substantially easier to raise money. And because the web is a useful tool for identifying fake projects and posers, a new tool for creating start-ups will be born.

Someone tried to launch a fake game on Kickstarter in April 2012 but got caught quickly. The ability to research the backgrounds of those posting projects and trying to get funding is only a click away. I'm sure there will be a high profile case of fraud, but I sure hope it doesn't shut this new financing conduit down. It is one thing to have some people lose a hundred dollars on an occasional bad Kickstarter project and a completely different thing to have Enron or Bernard Madoff take billions of dollars in a pyramid scheme and have investors lose their life savings.

It is hard to overestimate the importance of the development of crowdfunding as a source of early capital to start projects and launch companies. At TechShop, we have probably seen over 100 projects flow through, or touch, our locations on their way to Kickstarter success. We now teach classes on how to launch a successful Kickstarter project.

Danae Ringelmann, a founder at the international crowd-funding site Indiegogo, talks about the *five reasons* people invest. Only one of them is **profit**. This is important because the financial infrastructure and rules against advertising in the United States make it almost impossible to find people who will invest for the other four reasons. And people invest for portions of each: passion, participation, perks, pride, and, finally, profit:

- **Passion.** People love to invest time, money, and effort in things they are passionate about. Tom's Shoes comes to mind. You know, the company that gives away a pair of shoes to someone in the developing world every time you buy one. What a great idea. But if people were only interested in profit (what they were getting, monetarily, out of the deal), why would they pay more for a pair of shoes so that someone else would get a pair? Isn't that what charities are for?

- **Participation.** Many of the film projects on Indiegogo are funded because friends and family want to participate in some way in the project. They don't actually expect to get or be offered a return on their investment. They just want to support what a person they know is doing; they don't want to loan money; they don't want international royalty rights. They just want to participate.

- **Perks.** Hey, and by participating, these friends, family, acquaintances, and other investors might actually get to be an extra in that movie. Or they may get to be invited to the cast party, a special event, and/or dinner with the director. What do they care more about—the movie or hanging out at a party with the director and a bunch of movie folks? Is that worth $50 bucks, $100 bucks, maybe $500? Why not?
- **Pride.** I was pleased to see that pride was on Danae's list. Yes, one of the seven deadly sins is a motivator to invest. As is greed (profit). Who wouldn't want to help a successful restaurant come to your local neighborhood? Pride of helping the community by participating in local projects and events is a great motivator for those who know how to tap into it well.

Crowdfunding allows for the combination of reasons that people invest, and it makes it possible for projects and investors to find each other.

Another new friend, Dan Miller, recently launched Fundrise.com, a real estate crowdfunding site, with his brother. The idea here is that locals invest together in local real estate, thus potentially controlling the nature of the development in their neighborhoods. Do people invest for profit? Sure they do, but they also want to participate in their local community; they are passionate about the types of businesses that are on the corner. They take pride in owning a piece of the neighborhood and might get a few perks from the local restaurant that moved in because the landlord (they) leaned into the project and cut a budding restaurateur a great lease.

This is not the same thing as a real estate investment trust (REIT), a security that sells like a stock on Wall Street and invests in *real estate* directly. This is local ownership with pride and passion. This is crowdfunding at its best. And it is radically different from pure development.

ALIBABA

If you are about to use Kickstarter to get going, then it may be time to look into manufacturing in volume offshore. Now, as you can probably tell by the tone of this book, I prefer to see manufacturing closer to the market. But the reality of international commerce and economics is such that it is often just plain cheaper to get a product made overseas. Particularly in developed categories with low margins, one has to squeeze as much cost out as possible. Setting up one's own manufacturing plant in the early stages of growth may not make sense. It may never make sense. But many of the Kickstarter projects I've seen are potential candidates for finding contract manufacturing around the world.

Once again, the Internet comes to save the day. A Chinese Internet company, Alibaba.com, a global e-commerce platform that connects buyers and suppliers around the world, is like the eBay of global contract manufacturing. It is possible to have just about anything made for extremely competitive prices. This is where China really does shine. It's not just that the Chinese can do it cheaply, it's that they have a very dense network of suppliers who carry almost everything and short, tight supply chains that can get the rest. The number and variety of flexible manufacturers in China with access to the hardest-to-find components means the job can be done quickly and cheaply and you can have it drop-shipped to your door anywhere in the world. This is the true competitive advantage that China has developed: there is no place else in the world where anything can be made, in volume, quickly, and very inexpensively. Some of the world's best manufacturing capabilities are now only a click away.

ETSY

I met Christopher Steinrueck of Wood Thumb at Maker Faire 2011 in San Mateo, California. We gave him some space in the TechShop area where we were showcasing what some of our members were making. Christopher makes wooden ties— ones that go around the neck, not ones on a railroad. He scavenges deadwood and reclaimed wood from barns, the beach, or reclamation centers. He then creates custom, or bespoke, ties from the wood.

I admit, I had a hard time understanding why someone would want to make wooden ties—but then I saw them. They are beautiful. I was a little dubious he'd sell very many, but Father's Day was coming up, so maybe he'd sell a few.

Boy, was I wrong. Christopher sold out his entire inventory by lunch on the first day. He ran back to the shop to make as many more as he could before the next day, and then spent the rest of the faire taking orders and promising to have them ready for Father's Day. Then he learned about Etsy, a website where people sell handmade or vintage items.

Etsy is wonderful for creating a market for people who make things by hand. There is a big social component to what Etsy does. The site makes it easy for users to set up an Etsy store, and it provides online tutorials, a community of store owners, and now even regional meetups and fairs. People who make things by hand have now found an online market designed for them. It isn't eBay; it's a social store for crafters and makers to meet and sell products that they have made to their customers and, in many instances, their customers' families and friends. It is a great way to reach out across the Internet and reach the friends of friends of friends, strangers who are actually within your broader network. This happens through "likes" on Facebook, retweets on Twitter, and even through e-mail, personal websites, or PR. Etsy has created a fabulous global following by enabling people like Christopher to quickly and easily set up a web store and find customers around the world.

I didn't buy a tie from Christopher that weekend, but I now own a beautiful redwood tie, I bought my father one, and I purchased a wooden bow tie for my son. I ordered them from the ThinkGeek catalog for Christmas. Sweet. As for Christopher, he went from budding entrepreneur at his first fair to being distributed through online and offline catalogs. Another lifestyle business built through a combination of online tools and access to physical tools.

YES & YES DESIGNS

Laura Bruland of Yes & Yes Designs is another of my favorites. She is a great example of the potentially liberating power of the combination of these new economic forces at play. I met Laura for the first time in 2011, about the same time I met Christopher. I believe she used to be a barista, though she was so focused on her art that she had little interest in talking about her day job. However, she was happy to tell me about her weekend sport as "Chiquita Bonanza," a member of the Bay Area Derby Girls roller derby team.

I like to joke with Laura about her "hatred" for books because she rips the covers off them and then tortures the hardback covers with lasers. Well, not really. Laura loves books, but she does use discarded, outdated book covers to make custom jewelry with the laser cutter. Like many artists, once she was shown all that a laser cutter could do, she was off and running.

In her own words, Laura makes "bold and one-of-a-kind jewelry from recycled books." It is beautiful. Laura sells mostly earrings, necklaces, and pins, all of which have something of 1950s vintage feel to them. She, too, came to the Maker Faire and has been doing weekend shows and building her business. TechShop featured her in an advertisement, and Wired.com featured her in the "Wired Design" section. She quickly learned about Etsy, set up a store, and began promoting herself online as well as at the weekend events.

About a year later, Laura was so busy she was running up against our shop's limits on the amount of time one can use the laser cutter (we are good for short runs, but you can't set up a manufacturing center). She wasn't sure what to do but then hit on the idea of launching a Kickstarter campaign to raise enough money to buy her own laser cutter. "I need a laser cutter. I will name her Lucky," it says on her campaign page. Well, Laura raised over $8,000 and bought herself a laser cutter. Yes & Yes Designs is now in 25 retailers around the world, including the San Francisco Museum of Modern Art store.

WHAT ARE YOU WAITING FOR?

Wooden ties, furry hats, book cover art, watches, iPad covers, iPhone covers, robots, furniture, clothing, jewelry. What are you waiting for? Surely you have some ideas. Or maybe you know someone with ideas. I am convinced commerce is shifting in some important ways and a lot more people are going to be able to participate in a personal way. More people are going to want to participate in a more personal way.

CNC mills, laser cutters, waterjet cutters, 3D printers, 123D Make modeling software. What are you waiting for? Some of these tools are stunningly easy to use, are a lot of fun, and can add depth to the relationships in your life if you use them to create gifts.

Entrepreneurs, artists, tinkerers, makers, crafters, engineers, architects. What do you want to be? Whom do you want to hang out with? What are you waiting for?

Yes. This is a revolution. This book is a manifesto. It can change your life. And, yes, I'm inviting you to become a revolutionary.

STARTUP WEEKEND

Startup Weekend is a nonprofit organization based in Seattle that creates and hosts weekend events where the objective is to pitch ideas to potential investors and to have the nascent beginning of a start-up at the end of the weekend. The process of setting up a weekend starts a couple of months before the event with announcement of the weekend coming to a particular city, sponsors being identified, mentors, judges, and angel investors recruited, and a small pool of funding made available as prize money.

A call then goes out for applicants. Most of the applicants are software focused, some with a physical product overlay—medical apps, social apps, or other such designations. Small teams form and submit a basic proposal. The proposal doesn't have to be well developed; the idea is to help develop it during the weekend to a point where a pitch to investors can be made. The event organizers then do a quick filter to make sure the highest-quality ideas and teams will be included, and then invitations are sent to selected applicants. This is a fairly standard approach to these types of boot camps and start-up weekends.

Note that the purpose of these weekends is to find big hits, not lifestyle businesses. There is nothing in Startup Weekend's charter that says it has to go for big hits, but because there are angels and committees involved, lifestyle businesses really need not apply. So Laura from Yes & Yes, Paul Youngblood of One Degree, Jazz Tigan of Hugalopes, and Perrin Lam the jeweler need not apply. There really should be start-up weekends for these kinds of entrepreneurs, too.

The teams show up on Friday, socialize, get to know one another, meet the mentors, and make a short pitch. There is some mix and match that then goes on—in the better-run versions, a couple of potentially hard-to-find skills are brought in, often identified in the submission process, like programmers (there are never enough programmers to go around at these events), financial modelers, user interface designers (not enough of them either)—and then the break until Saturday morning.

On Saturday, things start in earnest. Lots of brainstorming, ideas, market research, mentor meetings, and coffee. A basic outline of the weekend is adhered to with late afternoon or early evening pitches to the mentors, some basic mock-ups of the app, product, or service, questions, and pushback. All of this is followed by a long night of reworking ideas, building mock-ups, and working on the pitches.

Sunday, if everything has gone well, and it often has not, the idea is refined, basic mock-ups are done, and a deck is created to pitch from. Late Sunday afternoon, the angels and judges arrive, kibitz a bit, socialize with the teams (though not much, because the teams are focused), and then the pitches happen. At the close of Sunday, the winners are awarded, angels talk to individual teams, and the weekend is wrapped up.

There are few objectives with this approach. The first, obviously, is to identify great ideas and great teams and get them working together on an idea. The second is to expose these teams and ideas to angels and other entrepreneurs. A third objective is to create interest in the entire idea of purposeful innovation, where teams come together specifically to find a problem and then solve it. There are other objectives, like exposing entrepreneurs to rapid prototyping, exposing budding entrepreneurs to the start-up culture, getting local companies, foundations, and governments more actively engaged in the local start-up community, and enticing the press to cover the local start-up community. But the real idea is to help kick-start some start-ups.

One of the great things about Startup Weekend is that, with the Kauffman Foundation's support, the nonprofit has been able to bootstrap itself to a place where it now holds hundreds of these weekend events all over the globe.

Another nice thing about this platform is that the restriction of accepting only software ideas into the start-up pool is slowly being lifted with the recognition that hardware start-ups are getting easier and less expensive to fund, develop, and launch.

Events like these start-up weekends are critical for the development of local entrepreneurial talent. Many universities now conduct similar events, and some foundations and other sponsors are holding them all over the globe.

OPEN INNOVATION

I would be remiss not to mention another trend called open innovation. Over a decade ago, economist and professor Dr.

Eric von Hippel[1] of MIT wrote a book, *Democratizing Innovation*, that broke open the discussion on the origin of innovative ideas. In this seminal work, von Hippel cited studies that he and his graduate students conducted that indicated that over half of useful innovations came from heavy users (lead users), not the research and development departments or customer insight departments in large companies. These weren't just any old ideas, but actually fully functioning modifications to existing products to better meet the users' needs. This goes beyond listening to your customers for great ideas, this goes to licensing the good ideas your customers have perfected.

Around the same time, another professor, Dr. Henry Chesbrough, wrote *Open Innovation*.[2] This book identified specific pathways that organizations could use to engage customers, researchers, and developers outside the normal reach of a research and development organization.

With the proof points from von Hippel and pathways developed by Chesbrough, a small group of firms has emerged that help large firms systematize the way to bring in ideas. Procter & Gamble embraced these ideas early on and has had a number of wins by using the processes. DARPA is using these methods to explore how to cut the costs on developing major platforms. An online game was even developed by one group working on difficult problems around folding proteins. The molecular structure of proteins is what makes many drugs work. Proteins are folded back on themselves in what looks like knots to the untrained eye. These folded proteins in many instances cannot yet be modeled, or solved, by computers. But it turns out that some people—special people sometimes with no special training, degrees, or background in biomedicine—seem to have a knack for visualizing folding patterns in three-dimensional space. So by creating a game and tapping the expertise of this particular crowd, researchers have been able to solve key protein folding problems in a fraction of the time.

Some of the success of the open innovation, open source, and hardware movements is being driven by democratizing access to formerly incredibly expensive tools. Open innovation drives down the costs of innovation.

Because of all these trends, open innovation and open source, along with the new cheap access to capabilities, there is an opportunity to remake at least a portion of how a company does some of its new product development. Innovations no longer should or need to all come out of a company's R&D labs; there are more "lead users" (von Hippel's term) with deeply informed and sometimes patentable ideas out in diaspora than a firm will ever be able to employ internally. Creating the on-ramps for these outside sources of innovation is critical to the competitive position and survival of large firms.

TOWARD A TWO-WEEK INTERVENTION

My company has wanted to develop a two-week version of the Start-up Weekend for corporations where we spend the first week developing what the product should be and the second week launching the product. One way of launching would be to use Kickstarter or Indiegogo as the go-to market solution. If you can't get the product funded on the crowdsourcing platform, you kill the idea and then try again.

Imagine a team from a packaged goods company, film studio, or clothing company actually funding the development of the business's product through the crowd instead of with a budget from the stage-gated new product development process. If the team gets $1 million in orders from the campaign, how is the division's general manager not going to listen to the team?

I've proposed that some of these Fortune 500 firms should be launching a product a week using this method. It's cheaper, faster, and more accurate than doing traditional marketing activities. This doesn't necessarily mean they need to eliminate the standard new product development process, just that it needs to be augmented.

I feel sorry for the dinosaurs that don't begin to experiment with these new ways of testing and launching products.

THE FUTURE OF VENTURE CAPITAL

The current system of venture capital first developed in the 1960s has evolved into a focus on home runs. This is to some extent driven by the boom and bust nature of the businesses companies are in, the IPO market cycles or "window" as it's called, but to a significant extent it has been the result of a series of actions taken by Congress and the SEC (Securities and Exchange Commission) to reduce fraud perpetuated by Enron and other scandals. The 2002 Sarbanes-Oxley Act's rules for auditing added over $1 million in annual costs for even small firms to comply. As a by-product of our fears related to fraud, we have managed to utterly destroy the IPO market for companies under $50 million in sales. "Destroy" is not too strong a term. There has been a 90 percent reduction in the number of these IPOs in the last couple of decades.[3] How would you feel if you lost 92 percent of your food? The U.S. regulatory regime has basically been doing that to the American economy—starving it.

According to a Kauffmann study, all of the new jobs in the U.S. economy were produced by start-ups in the last few decades. They call them gazelles, very fast start-ups growing quickly. Corporate America sheds jobs, merges and cuts jobs, automates and eliminates jobs, and the new jobs net are created by start-ups. And we had made it almost impossible to fund smallish, interesting start-ups because one of the key sources of funding, venture capital, couldn't get small exits. They have been forced to swing for the fences. Basically, if a group can't tell a VC (venture capital) or angel group with a straight face that its idea could be a $1 billion exit, they aren't very interested in it. Even if you show a VC or angel group a $100-million-a-year market that, if everything works out, you could dominate, it will pass. It's too risky, and the only exit is through a private equity firm or acquisition.

That changed in 2012. With the passage of the JOBS Act, Sarbanes-Oxley was waived for smaller firms. This has yet to play out with the venture capital firms, but there is now room for multiple investments where the strategy is small hits instead of home runs. Exits are in the $50 million to $100 million range. It will take more deals and a different process, but this is a potential sea change. And that's nothing compared to the potential tsunami coming from the illumination of advertising for securities.

JOBS ACT IMPACT ON RAISING MONEY FOR START-UPS

Ever since the early 1930s, companies and individuals in the United States have not been allowed to raise money through advertising. The purpose of this was to protect investors from losing their money. It successfully cut down on the proliferation of scams, but it also put a huge clamp on start-up funding. Consequently, liquidity in the market for start-ups dried up.

I remember the first time I ran into this back in the 1980s. I was trying to raise money for a great idea, adding audio capability to computers. I asked the attorney for the company I worked with whether I could post the idea and raise money on computer bulletin boards. I was pretty sure there were plenty of early PC geeks who would have loved to invest in the idea. I think he laughed at me.

"You will go to jail if you do that," he said. I had to use family and friends, a bank, or a venture capitalist.

My friends were all starving students, so I had to use family and their friends. I had to go out, get introductions, and meet my potential investors face-to-face. This was stunningly inefficient compared to my plan of launching a campaign on a bulletin board.

Well, 30 years later, the federal regulatory regime is finally about to join the latter part of the twentieth century. Legislation should have been changed by now, and we could have done it and done it well decades ago, but at least Congress is getting to it now. At the time of this writing, we are waiting for the final rules to be issued. Once they do get issued, we will be able to have Kickstarter-like portals for raising capital for start-ups. This will be much more efficient than the current process. And if the company is raising less than $1 million, it can take a limited amount of money from anyone. This could actually change everything for start-ups in the United States. The timing is perfect for the Maker Movement. Right as the spread of knowledge and hardware tools develops, raising money may become easier than it ever has been.

The traditional approach to funding these small start-ups has been family and friends or maybe credit cards, second mortgages, and raiding the 401(k). But not anymore. If the idea has merit, it is likely to be funded. We might even see a lot of local investing going on. You want to start a restaurant? Great. Get your friends and family to vouch for you and launch your offer online. You can do equity and loans this way. Think about the great chefs in various cities who could open their own restaurants if they simply had access to the capital they needed. Yes, there are downsides, but fear of those downsides has almost totally destroyed entrepreneurial opportunity in the United States. Currently, if you don't have a strong balance sheet, income, a rich uncle, or lots of wealthy friends, then there is no rung on the ladder for you. You have to go work for the man because you aren't going to get the conservative capital people to fund you—ever.

It is time to put the twentieth century behind us and use the Internet, the crowd, and crowdfunding to find the new winners. Lowering the bar to entrepreneurialism is the most liberating, democratizing, and just thing that can done for those who are creative, bold, and daring enough to trust their talents and try.

6

Democratization of Tools and Information

■ ■ ■

TOOLS

Since the beginning of the industrial revolution until fairly recently, the most powerful tools of production were centralized. With the advent of capitalism and the need to control large sums of money to leverage industrialization, many segments of the economy that previously had been serviced by individuals began to give way to industrial capitalists. This is not a bad thing; huge improvements in lifespan, living conditions, workweeks, and lifestyles have resulted from industrialization and mechanization. Bad things happened, too, though most of us would not trade our era for that of 1850, in which we would likely be farmers with a life expectancy of 36.9 years and work 12-hour days in a six- or seven-day workweek.

Until very recently, the tools of creation and production in many fields have remained the purview of those with access to capital. In the last 20 years, however, something very interesting has happened with the democratization of computers, computer power, and the Internet. In practical terms, the cost of launching a software company has dropped at least a couple orders of magnitude. The amazing development of the open source software community, where software is free to use, where upgrades to the software are required to be shared, and where development is free for everyone has been nothing short of revolutionary. With the continued drop in the costs of processing, companies are now being created for tens of thousands of dollars instead of tens of millions.

In 2000, during the dot-com craze, I was working as the COO on a start-up with a $30 million hardware and software budget before we even went live. Today, with the advent of the LAMP (Linux, Apache, MySQL, and the PHP programming language) stack, now combined with cloud computing, where you pay only for the cycles you use, start-ups are getting going for $25,000 to $150,000. Not all, of course, but lots. This has famously led to an explosion of new web-based companies that have changed the way we live, shop, and consume.

More slowly, the same kind of thing has been happening on the hardware side. It has gotten cheaper, more powerful, and easier to use. Better, faster, cheaper has jumped to hardware.

CHEAPER

The core technology for creating prototypes is the mill and lathe. These are hard-core industrial technologies that were rarely seen outside of a production facility. Few were in the hands of basic consumers, and they cost tens of thousands of dollars, sometimes $100,000. They required three-phase power, not something most households had in their garages. They required years of use to become expert at and therefore were only used by professionals. Then the Japanese came along and wiped out much of the capital tool manufacturing base in the United States. The Chinese came in behind them and destroyed much of the Japanese base. And now anyone can buy a basic mill or lathe for less than $10,000 with a digital readout (DRO).

You see, a few decades ago machine manufacturers started to add DROs to these machines to help machinists do their work without having to constantly use mechanical measurement devices. These DROs were expensive, though— $100,000 each in some cases. But today the machine purchaser basically gets them free. So, a $10,000 mill today comes with what would have been a $100,000 DRO not long ago.

POWERFUL

Starting in the mid-1950s, thanks to some work at MIT, we saw the development of computer numerical controlled (CNC) machines. These could read digital code and control the cutting tool directly with minimal human intervention. This is truly an amazing development and has led to what is being described as "lights out manufacturing." A CNC tool doesn't need light to see. It just does what the computer code tells it to do. Nothing more, nothing less. I'm skipping over a lot of development work here, but the reality is that you can now deploy dozens of machines, working 24-7, creating thousands of things with minimal inputs of labor. The Chinese are far more concerned about the impact of robotics on their labor advantage than they are about companies shifting production to India or Vietnam.

CNC robots change the nature of production profoundly. Again, there has been a huge drop in prices and an incredible improvement in ease of use. As recently as 2000, a basic CNC software seat could run $100,000. In addition, a machinist would have had to learn how to program in G-code, an esoteric system for controlling a cutting edge in three-dimensional space, as well as know geometry and some calculus, and then go through a solid six months of training on the software to become good at it. Consequently, a couple of years of training or time at a trade school were still required in order to use these tools effectively. But now, it's possible to purchase stand-alone packages for $1,500 or so. And the more popular packages are typically bundled with the machine for free.

CNC tools would run hundreds of thousands of dollars and require years of experience and training to be useful. Now they are much cheaper; anyone can get them for about $20,000, and a very nice entry-level, multi-tool-changing machine from Haas sells for under $50,000 brand new. Just as important, these machines have become easier to use.

EASY

Now for the magic: software to do it all. Inexpensive or free design software from Autodesk and other providers now allows novices to leverage the power of the industrial revolution with their personal computer, something they already own. Even better, they can begin to learn how to use these tools this week. At TechShop, we are teaching the basics of these tools in a few class sessions and then watching our members go out on the machines and make useful things. This is stunning. We run people through their own industrial revolution in weeks instead of years or decades. They are using these newfound tools to completely remake themselves—and, in some instances, take on large Fortune 500 companies head to head.

IMPLICATIONS

Cheap and powerful drive revolutions; cheap, powerful, and easy to democratize them. As a new product development professional, I know that all large firms have the equivalent of a stage-gated new product development process. They have anywhere from a low of 5 stages to a high of 20 or more stages. I ran one with 7:

1. **Cloud of possibilities.** This included exploration, futures work, patent tracking, and benchmarking. It was formless and nebulous and hated.
2. **Ideation.** Out of the cloud of external and internal ideas, one comes up with long lists of things that might or could be made.
3. **Screening.** There has to be a filter against which you bounce the ideas.
4. **Research.** Ask questions like, is there a market, can it be made using existing technology, what else is needed, should we do this?
5. **Development.** Develop preproduction prototypes for testing, refinement, market research, and beta customer feedback.
6. **Manufacturing.** Build and sell the product or service.
7. **Analysis and feedback.** The most commonly forgotten part of the process—analyze what have we learned.

To send an idea through this entire process took months, sometimes years, and usually cost millions of dollars. It is stage-gated in that at every step there is a formal review and a go/no-go decision. We added a few innovative twists, we had a rapid development track, we had some people with resurrection power (the ability to fund something killed outside the normal channels), and we had a general manager who could even pull a rabbit out of his hat by fully funding an entire cycle inside of one fiscal year, thereby creating something out of nothing by burying development in a sales budget and skipping the entire process (this is not for the faint of heart). To the uninitiated, it sounds crazy, but it is necessary. Entire books have been written on the process, PhDs have been awarded; a large organization with the acronym of PDMA (Product Development Management Association) is dedicated to it.

This is what the software development cycle looked like back in the days of the mainframe. This is not how a lot of software is developed today. Some still is—operating systems from Microsoft, for example. Major upgrades to Word or PowerPoint require lots of work, lots of meetings, lots of features, and debates on what shade of loam green to use and how tightly spaced an apostrophe should be from an *s*.

But that isn't how Twitter, Facebook, or Instagram were launched, for two basic reasons. The first is cost. If there isn't a lot at risk, you don't need big teams costing hundreds of thousands or millions of dollars reviewing every decision. Building a software company doesn't take much of anything now. Today, even Facebook would only cost a fraction of what it cost when it was launched.

Second, these start-ups were being driven by an end-user entrepreneur. End-user entrepreneurs don't need or use stage-gated review processes to launch their products. They use themselves or a small group in their "kitchen cabinet" to guide development. This saves an incredible amount of time and money.

Some important things start to happen when you can seed a software company for $25,000. First, you can take more bets, however unlikely. If one needed $500,000 to $1,000,000 in 2005 to fund a start-up and $5 million to $50 million in 2000, there were just plain fewer bets made. For the cost to bet on one idea in 2000, you can now make hundreds of bets. This is why we are seeing an explosion of mobile, social, and gaming app development in nearly every incubator in the world. And now there are incubators, it seems, in nearly every city in the world. If your city doesn't have an incubator, start one. It's cheaper than it has ever been, and everyone is doing it. Even phone companies are now starting incubators. It's a little crazy, as most incubators have failed. However, failing is getting cheaper, so the risk-to-reward ratio is turning in the favor of the incubators.

Another important thing to note is that we are still in the early days of the mobile computer and smartphone ecosystem. So there is more opportunity today to start a company, there are fewer entrenched competitors, and there is more experimentation happening than ever before. This is all good for creating early wins.

But that is software. I'm interested in hardware. Here is the magic: I mentioned in an earlier chapter that the same thing that has enabled the explosion of software incubators is starting to happen on the hardware side. Access to the tools of the industrial revolution is increasing, the costs of designing and developing product are dropping, the knowledge and skill required to design are dropping, the ability to access markets through the Internet has never been easier, and the funding mechanisms are becoming easier to access through places like AngelList (https://angel.co) Indiegogo, and Kickstarter. We have begun to see a significant uptick in incubator start-ups being hardware companies—from essentially zero a few years ago to 15 to 20 percent of them today.

We will talk about Local Motion in a later chapter, but it is an example of a hardware-focused start-up.

I haven't met Paul Youngblood yet, but he works out of our San Jose location. He is an award-winning designer by training, I would guess in his late twenties to early thirties. Paul recently successfully completed a Kickstarter campaign to start a watch company. He needed $15,000 and pulled in more than $25,000. I bought one of his watches during his campaign, a One Degree (his brand name) "I left my heart in San Francisco" watch. It is beautiful. Paul used 3D printing technology to do all the modeling, the laser cutter to make some templates, and other machines to get his design exactly the way he wanted it. He bought the movements from a Swiss movement company and the components from China, and then he assembled the watches, packaging and shipping them himself on our tables in San Jose. Paul now plans to offer the watches more broadly and will begin working on an "I Love NY" line.

A decade ago, it was not possible to start a designer watch company for $25,000. No one is likely to get an angel group or venture capital company to fund a watch company. Yet for a mere $25,000 Paul Youngblood started, launched, and delivered the first 100 watches from his new company.

How did he do it? He had a big leg up as he was a watch producer to begin with, but the real key was access to designer software, Autodesk Inventor, and the tools, 3D printers, lasers, mills, and lathes, combined with a supply chain reaching out to China and Switzerland that was ready, willing, and able to deal with units as low as 100. He had access to the hardware platform he needed to get started. With social media like

Facebook and Twitter and a crowdfunding platform of Kickstarter or Indiegogo, he was off and running. He didn't need to use his credit card to get started. He used the wisdom of the crowds, his skills, and a makerspace's hardware platform.

It is hard to overestimate the importance of access to tools. The early adherents of Marx were tradespeople and unions that were seeing the balance of power shifting from them to those who could afford industrial machine tools. It was a bloody time. But people felt so strongly about having personal access to tools that they supported the insanity that became the social and political oppression of communism. As it turns out, the medicine in this instance was worse than the disease, but let me restate what I just said: *People died to try to maintain their personal access to the tools of production.*

I like to say that I grade our Dream Consultants on how well they lead tours of our facilities. I don't actually grade them, but it is instructive to remind them of how important those tours are to our visitors. So they get a C if someone signs up for a class or becomes a member after a tour. With the exception of those from out of town who are just touring the facility because they love the idea of it (almost half of our tours are currently for out-of-towners—we should probably open a restaurant and bar!), most folks who walk through the door for a tour are predisposed to buy something. They have taken time for a 15- to 20-minute tour of a fabrication studio. They want something. Staff members get a B if they get a hug from the total stranger that they just met and spent 15 minutes with. Even if you are not a "huggy" person—and I am not a huggy person—you will end up giving (and getting) a lot of hugs. Most tours end with a B.

So, how do you get an A following a TechShop tour? You bring tears to the eyes of the visitor. This happens all the time.

Imagine that you just received your master's degree in art or mechanical engineering. After a decade of effort through high school, college, and graduate school, you have been working diligently in the schools' labs, studios, and work spaces on projects that were dictated to you at some level—and then, when you are finally getting good at what you've been doing, you graduate, they give you a diploma, and they take away access to the very labs that lift your spirits every day. You are sent out into the world to ply your trade—without the tools to do it. You are lost without tools. So, you get a job to either fund your need for tools or as a professional in your field meaning that you "get" to continue to work on stuff that other people think is important. Imagine the wonderful day you find a membership-based workshop that charges about three dollars a day, less than the cost of a single class for a single semester at most universities in the United States, and you take a tour with someone who is as passionate about making things as you are. Yes, you would likely tear up too.

I'm still not very comfortable giving hugs, but I've stopped fighting them. The breakthrough came one day when our team was in Vancouver, British Columbia, a few years ago. We had given a presentation to a group about what we were doing and why we thought it was so important. One of the people in the audience insisted on taking us to lunch so he could have his wife come downtown and meet us. So we went out to lunch. His wife came, and we talked at length about what we were doing and about access to tools, community, and information. As we were getting ready to leave, the wife, with tears in her eyes, insisted on hugging each of us. She implored us to keep fighting and to extend the reach of the platform.

It was not the first time this had happened to me, but it was just so startling. I didn't know these people, had never met them before, and in just 30 minutes we had gotten to the place where one of them was ready to cry for joy. Maybe physicians deal with this, and I should start to wear a white lab coat to fend people off with. No, I've stopped fighting hugs. Yes, people do cry when you tell them they can have access to the tools, information, and community they need to pursue and achieve their dreams.

OPEN SOURCE HARDWARE

The open source hardware effort is driving down the costs of the hardware. Arduino is probably the most famous of the efforts; the founders have become minicelebrities in the maker community. Arduino is an open source community for the development, extension, and improvement of an open microcontroller platform. What this means is that no one has the exclusive rights or owns the intellectual property for the platform. It is given away. It is owned by everyone and no one.

A microcontroller is a silicon chip that can be programmed to control things like sensors, switches, and other devices. It is a combination of software and hardware, and its development is shepherded by the community. If you use it and extend its functionality, you are required to document that functionality and donate that intellectual property back to the Arduino community.

Because it is not owned by anyone, developers who work on the project are coding and developing for the good of the community and their reputations in the community. Lots of developers have jumped on board. One of the benefits is that the software is free and the hardware is cheap. This makes it one of the cheapest platforms on which to develop prototypes. Also, by design, the software is relatively easy to learn. On the down side, there is a lot of "overhead" or bulk to using this kind of general microcontroller for prototyping, and even though an Arduino board may only cost $30 or so, a truly inexpensive, specifically designed microcontroller chip can cost just pennies. But you have to be able to code it in assembly language or some other low-level (read harder to program) language.

One of the things that makes the Arduino so cool is that it is easy to use and it is supported by a huge community of people who have shared their projects. So you can download code and plans for robots, planes, remote controlled vehicles, drones, sprinkler controllers. The list is almost endless. Another great thing is that the Arduino platform lowers the barrier to prototyping, so someone who is not a software programming expert can code something up from scratch even though he or she may not be a microcontrol programmer by training. TechShop's Radio Frequency Identification (RFID) system was prototyped by our founder in a couple of weeks on an Arduino board. We use it for checking out machines and getting into the shop. Once we had the functionality we wanted, we moved the RFID system to a PIC processor, which is much cheaper to deploy (and harder to program) than Arduino's.

Open source hardware is truly huge. With a little bit of effort and training, you can make your own electronic things. And you don't need $100,000 of design software, manufacturing experience, or years of dedicated software training. If you don't want to develop using the Arduino platform, it's possible to hire people for a reasonable rate to do the work for you, and they don't need to support hundreds of thousands of dollars of infrastructure costs. Arduino-based prototypes are also easy to change. They are fully programmable. So if the first effort doesn't work, you just keep hacking at the code until the device does what you want it to do.

Chris Anderson, formerly editor in chief of *Wired* magazine, quit his job to run his Arduino-based DIY drone company. For over a decade, he was arguably the leading commentator of the Internet, and he wrote a book, *The Long Tail* (which I mentioned in Chapter 3), that is probably the most important book about the impact of the Internet. He has been writing for over a decade about the stunning revolution that is the Internet and has written another book, *Makers: The New Industrial Revolution.*

Here is why I mention him: Chris Anderson quit his job to participate in the "new" revolution. He was not satisfied observing this revolution; he wanted to participate. In a recent talk at the Long Now Foundation titled "The Makers Revolution,"[1] he said, "If you thought the web was big, I think this [the new maker revolution] is going to be bigger." Again, this is from the number one chronicler of the Internet.

How could he say that? Think about it. The web is virtual. Admittedly, the virtual consumes more and more of my time, but *all* of my time is physical. Even when I'm online, I'm using a computer, phone, or tablet. I'm sitting in a chair, train, plane, or automobile. The web changed markets, sales, communication, democracy, politics, and more, but web was achieved through a screen. This new revolution is about materials, tools, physical communities, and bricks and mortar—the real world, or "RL" in Dungeons and Dragons gamer speak. RL is bigger and will always be bigger than the web. And access to RL is getting cheaper and easier. That is very big news indeed.

COMMUNITIES

At TechShop, we keep getting asked whether we have a virtual community of makers collaborating. We don't. We will someday. But we have something better. We have an actual physical community of makers exchanging ideas and working together. In a makerspace, you are two degrees of freedom away from success. That means you know someone (first degree) who knows someone (second degree) who can help you solve your current problem. Often, right now, and right where you are. Not a Google search, not e-mail, help, chat, or virtual assistance. This person can introduce you to another person who can come right next to you, someone who is ready, willing, and able to guide your hands.

We have found that something magical happens after about 300 people join a makerspace. Before that threshold, people come to the space because they have to use a tool in the space to get their project done. After about 300 members, the vibe in the community is so powerful that the mentality of the members switches such that they want to work on their projects in that space even if they don't need to use the tools. It becomes a true community where people help one another, care for one another, and hang out and socialize. It becomes a true third place. A place that isn't home or work, but a place where one can unwind, relax, and pursue a passion with like-minded creative people.

RESULTS

Max Gunawan became a TechShop member in 2012. He immediately started taking classes, including three different laser cutter classes in just a couple of months. Max is a designer by trade, so he comes to a makerspace with many basic skills already. All members bring some kind of assets with them when they look to launch their next thing. Max had worked at the Gap in its merchandising design group.

Max was inspirited by what he saw other members doing with their new access to tools, software, and the community, and he started to work on a unique lamp idea that he had.

By using the laser cutter to carve out sections of thin veneer wood, it is possible make what looks like a book cover. The spine is carved up to allow it to fold and bend over without stressing the wood. It is beautiful. With this basic design, Max began to experiment with paper substitutes to go inside the "book cover" that would create a nice glow when lit from behind. He eventually settled on Tyvek, a recyclable, translucent, durable plastic made by DuPont. Max glued the sheets of Tyvek together to make a fanlike structure that opens up when you open the cover.

Having signed up for a basic soldering class, Max was able to construct a simple on/off switch so that the lamp turns on when the "book" is opened. He sourced an LED light, a lithium ion battery, and then added some magnets, hidden into the cover, so that by using a supplied cord (with another magnet in it), the lamp can be easily hung or attached to the side of anything metal. This feature falls into the "customer surprise" category and is a wonderful touch.

Max has been working on his concept for months. He has leveraged the space nicely and used the access to the tools, the software, and the community well. The platform has enabled him to plug the gaps in his background (by taking classes and exchanging ideas with others in the community) and allowed him to build the prototypes himself for a nominal cost and use the software for design and actual manufacturing of the first short runs.

I met Max just a few weeks before his Kickstarter campaign. As he showed me his design, we talked about what a successful crowdfunding effort looked like and discussed his initial target of $60,000. That's actually pretty high for a crowdfunding effort. Current common wisdom is to target something around $4,000.

Max was adamant, though, having done his research on costs for each component in the right volumes to meet his price targets. He needed $60,000. Well, he funded that *in the first day*. With 10 days left, he hit $400,000, and he finished his campaign with $578,000.

When you combine cheap, easy, and powerful tools with the community, knowledge, and the desire to innovate, great new products are developed by amazing people. Dan and Roy Sandberg were two of TechShop's earliest members, joining in late 2006. They spent the next few years developing and perfecting their remote controlled video conferencing robot. The brothers did everything themselves, from the wiring harnesses and the electronics, including the gyros that controlled its balance, to the video conferencing software, power control, remote control software, mechanical engineering, and even the vacuum formed plastic enclosures. They were at the shop almost every day, working away on this breakthrough video conferencing program.

Walking down one of the halls, I met them for the first time when a five-foot-tall thingy came around the corner looking like a cross between a music stand, a Segway base, and a computer screen. On the screen was Dan's face. "Hi, I'm Dan," said Dan's disembodied face.

"Well, this isn't Dan," the disembodied face continued, "but I am . . ." He tried to explain the obvious, but confused it just a little bit more anyway.

"Hi, I'm Mark," I responded. "What is this thing?"

"It's a remote controlled video conference platform," Dan's voice said. "We call it the Giraffe because it has a really long neck. I'm controlling it from the room next door, but I could control it from anywhere there is an Internet connection."

At a loss for words, I just said, "Cool."

It isn't often you get to peer into a future a good 5, 10, or 15 years in advance, but it was obvious to me that I was doing just that.

The idea is simple: a device that you can control remotely, that runs a continuous video stream so you can roam around an office or factory on your own.

When I learned that Roy and Dan were working to keep the price point down to $5,000, I was stunned. I had heard of systems like this that were selling for $200,000. At the price point they were trying reach, they would be ubiquitous. Every office would want to have one to let remote workers "show up" to work. I quickly concluded that somewhere in the future, someone was going to have a meeting in which most, but not all, of the people "at" the meeting would be present through one of these robots. I haven't seen that yet, but it is only a matter of time.

At $5,000 apiece, I would have easily snuck 10 to 20 of these things into Avery Dennison when I worked there. With manufacturing plants and offices spread over 60 locations or more, having machines that executives, engineers, and HR folks could log into and drive around remotely would have been amazing. I remember one meeting in which a senior executive dispatched a team to Europe to find out about some issue, get it resolved, and get back within the week to report what happened. Imagine if they would have been able to walk away from that meeting, log into a squad of Giraffes, and start working right away. I'll bet they and their families would have been happier as well.

Dan and Roy eventually received a grant from a European agency to test the use of the Giraffe to help deliver low-level elderly care. In major cities, it turns out that a nurse can spend half his or her time commuting from one location to another.

If this device could be used to eliminate much if not all the driving, what would the impact be on the quality of the care both quantitatively and qualitatively? Often, innovations need that one application (the killer app for PCs was, famously, the spreadsheet) that will get them going, and this application (healthcare) seemed like a good one to the brothers—and they didn't have to give up ownership because it was a grant. They jumped on the opportunity, moved to Europe, and I didn't see them again for at least 18 months.

When I saw Dan at the end of 2012, I asked him how it was going. He said great, that they had sold their company and he was taking a sabbatical—for five years.

7

Rise of the Pro-Am

■ ■ ■

HUGALOPES

"Hi, Jazz," I said as I hit the top floor in our San Francisco location. I had met Jazz Tigan the previous month and had seen him just a week earlier working on a project.

Then I noticed he was in a leg cast. "Wow, what happened? How are you doing?"

"Well, Mark... actually... not so good. I had car problems on Monday, so I pulled out the bike yesterday to get here—and got hit by a car and broke my leg."

"Oh, no. That's a tough way to start any week!"

"Now I have to take the subway," he continued. "It stops just a couple of blocks away but, ouch, my arms are really sore from using these crutches." He paused. "But, hey, let me tell you about my project!"

Right in front of my eyes, Jazz's demeanor completely transformed. He went from discussing what I suspect will be one of the worst weeks of his life to a fully engaged and excited human about to share something special. Jazz is remarkable. I couldn't, however, get my mind off the car that hit him and broke his leg. I mean, this is California, where people sue one another practically for breathing.

"OK, OK, OK . . . uh, I'm working on my tagline. What do you think of this?" Jazz looked at me expectantly, a puppy-dog-like face eager for approval. "It's . . . a Mr. Potato Head for your . . . head!"

Silence.

Stunned silence.

This was bad on at least three levels. First, "Mr. Potato Head" is someone else's brand. You can't use someone else's brand in your tagline; you'll get sued, especially in California. Second, the visual image is not pretty. Have you seen Mr. Potato Head? This is a guy only Mrs. Potato Head could love. Third, if you are looking to make some quick money, I was thinking to myself, *sue the driver*. You know, the driver of the car that hit you and broke your leg.

Undaunted by my lack of enthusiasm for his tag line, Jazz added, "All right, follow me. I'll show you."

Hobbling to the fabric table where I could see a small mountain of very loud, brightly colored, furry fabric, Jazz set his crutches aside. Sneaking a look over his shoulder at me with an enthusiastic, "You are going to love this, I know it," he buried his head in the mountain of fur.

Just as quickly, Jazz whirled around, a furry monster with googly eyeballs, an enormous horn, and big red lips sitting askance on his head. Dangling around Jazz's shoulders were long, skinny, bright green, furry arms with mitten-like hands. Slipping his fingers into the gangly puppet/monster hat's hands, Jazz raised one and waved at me. In a childlike voice, he said, "Hi, Mark . . . Hiiiii, Maaaaark."

Sue the driver. That's the first thing that came into my head. Even after decades of new product training and experience where I know I'm not the customer (this is, like, rule number one for product managers: You are highly unlikely to be the perfect customer for the product you are developing. That is why we have human-centered design research, user groups, etc.), it is still hard not to viscerally react to a product or service.

"Let me show you how it works." Jazz switched to his normal voice. "You see here, inside, I have a patent-pending appliqué design so you can change out any of the parts. The eyes, ears, nose, arms, and horns can all be mixed and matched, just like Mr. Potato Head. I took the introduction to the patenting class you guys hold and filed a provisional patent. Then I used the red patent phone upstairs that you guys have set up to call the patent office to talk to my patent examiner, who told me he thought I could get a patent for my idea."

I was impressed. If you have a patent on something like this, I thought, you might actually be onto something, even if I wouldn't be caught dead in one.

"Next, I'm going to launch a Kickstarter campaign and see if I can raise enough money to go to the New York Toy Fair."

Going to the New York Toy Fair is another great idea; all the buyers from around the world show up, and if something is going to sell, it will sell there first.

"How much are you trying to raise?" I asked.

Jazz calculated that in order to cover the cost of the booth, materials, and "everything on the cheap," he and his partner needed to raise $8,500 on Kickstarter by selling early versions. "I'm going to launch next week. Would you tweet it when it comes out?"

"Of course," I said. "I would be glad to." It took all my self-control not to shake my head in dismay. A furry-monster-hat Mr. Potato Head? Jazz was doomed, I thought to myself.

I was wrong.

Jazz launched his Kickstarter campaign with his partner, Maricriz Perea, and they raised $21,000, far exceeding their $8,500 target. They went to the toy fair, met a bunch of people and companies, and licensed the product, which they dubbed Hugalopes, to Jakks Pacific, a top-five toy manufacturer.

Puppet Monsters, as the furry Hugalopes have come to be called, are sold through TV advertising, the "As Seen on TV" site, and the web for $19.95. I haven't seen Jazz recently, but I'm glad I kept my thoughts to myself and encouraged him to pursue his dream. I bought three for Christmas presents; they were big hits.

SQUARE

As we were moving into our second corporate location in San Francisco, as part the 5M Project, our founder Jim Newton told me that he was pretty sure that Square, the peer-to-peer merchant banking start-up started by Jack Dorsey, the founder of Twitter, had started at our location in Menlo Park. I wasn't so sure, as I had my office there as well and didn't remember seeing Jack Dorsey or Jim McKelvey on site. A quick review of our customer relationship manager (CRM) confirmed that, in fact, Jim McKelvey had been a member and taken some classes. Since then I've met Jim and heard Jack talk about our role in helping them launch.

There are some important lessons, I believe, to be learned from their journey. But first let's provide some background information. Jim McKelvey had spent the last 10 years running a successful glassblowing studio in St. Louis. It is a personal passion and interest of his and some friends. He had also had some great success with his interactive software media publishing company. Actually, that is where he and Jack had met. Jack had worked for him as an intern before going on to become an Internet titan through launching Twitter. But this is what is interesting, at least to this start-up junky:

Jim lost a commission on a beautiful custom faucet because he couldn't take American Express. He had been working with a woman in Latin America on a special design and lost the sale at the last minute because he couldn't take the right form of credit. He and Jack were friends and had been looking for a project to collaborate on.

Their idea was to use a smartphone and its platform as the communications and processing platform to initiate and conduct credit card purchases. This was an innovative idea, potentially very disruptive. They pulled together a presentation and, leveraging Jack's contacts in Silicon Valley, met with a handful of the top VC firms. They got absolutely nowhere—even with a social media genius opening the doors. But put yourself in the VC's shoes. Here were two young entrepreneurs, a coder (successful, but still a code jockey) and a glassblower, trying to convince potential investors that they were going to take on Wells Fargo, Chase, and Bank of America and target a segment of the market that none of the banks were interested in, namely, low-volume, higher-risk, mom-and-pop lemonade stands. They were turned down flat.

Jack and Jim didn't give up. They decided they needed to build a prototype. Jack wanted to use the camera on an iPhone to capture the number and name, while Jim felt it would be too hard to control for the light and would create a semi-permanent record of a card and that it would be better to develop a simple magnetic stripe reader. Jim's design won out, and it is actually a nice hack. Apple doesn't give out an API for its connector to the phone, but the microphone jack could be hacked to capture the simple magnetic stripe tones to grab a credit card's name and account number.

Jim came into our Menlo Park location, took a couple of classes, and in a matter of months had gone through three full generations of prototypes. Jack focused on the code. Then they rescheduled meetings with some VCs in the Valley. This is the coolest part of the story: The two walked into the meeting with a fully functional prototype. They asked for the VC's personal credit card, ran it through their system, raised their first $500 doing demonstrations, and then famously never gave the money back. Jack and Jim raised a $10 million series A off the strength of the demonstration prototype. According to Michael Arrington on CrunchBase, Square was valued at "a massive $40 million or more after raising $10 million in funding, and the service is yet to launch publicly for anyone to use."[1]

At the time of this writing, Square had a $3.25 billion market valuation and has raised over $300 million in capital. The company employs 400 people in downtown San Francisco and at the end of 2012 was running at an annualized rate of $6 billion in transactions. Square is rumored to be hiring 700 more people in 2013 and will do more than $30 billion in transactions.

Starbucks just signed up as a user and distributor of the Square devices. I see television commercials for them when I turn on the TV. Most important, Square destroyed the huge barriers to entry that the merchant banks had raised to deny entrepreneurs from accepting credit cards. Besides charging less than most of the merchant banks, Square dropped all the crazy requirements.

The last time I had a credit card terminal, I had to pay $125 a month for the "privilege" of renting a terminal so that my bank could extract 3.75 percent of every transaction—and on major transactions where the bank determined there might be a higher risk, it would charge me more. To get that terminal, I had to provide three years of financials, demonstrate a clean credit history, and have a strong balance sheet.

As a direct result of these kinds of fees, charges, and paperwork, vendors at local swap meets would not and could not take credit cards, nor could most independent taxi drivers, many bakers, cleaners, or anyone who had experienced a financial crisis in the last three years. Jack Dorsey and Jim McKelvey busted open the merchant banking oligopoly and let anyone with a smartphone and checking account take plastic. There are now literally lemonade stands that take plastic. And why not?

Let me replay this story more succinctly. A glassblower (successful and a smart entrepreneur, but a glassblower nonetheless) and a thirtysomething code jockey CEO created a multibillion-dollar merchant bank in three years, took on the largest financial institutions in the world, and crushed them. But it worked only because they had a fully functional prototype. Don't lose that. Jack was turned down until he had a prototype. If *you* don't have a prototype, good luck.

PRO-AM

These two very different examples, Hugalopes and Square, share some interesting characteristics. An important one is that neither set of entrepreneurs was an industry player in the industry being targeted. Jazz had never licensed a toy before, and Jack and Jim had zero experience in merchant banking. I met someone recently who had been at an early Square roadshow for banking industry players. She told me that more than half of those in attendance clearly didn't think Jim and Jack had a prayer of succeeding. Some did, but most did not. They were pro-ams, very talented amateurs getting ready to go professional in their field, but very definitely not professionals.

Neither had any domain expertise whatsoever. You don't expect an amateur to win big, but sometimes they do.

Both of these instances are examples of the triumph of the amateur. You can't stay an amateur, but just because you are not an industry player doesn't rule you out.

Jazz, Jack, and Jim learned the skills they needed as they went along—just-in-time skills and knowledge in product and business development. Elon Musk has been doing the same thing for his entire career as the cofounder of the money-transfer service PayPal; founder, product architect, and CEO of Tesla Motors, the electric car company; and founder of the rocket ship company SpaceX. He has always been an industry outsider who climbs whatever steep mountains of knowledge are needed for each venture. Very few of the industry players in either domain would have bet on Elon. He may still fail, but his companies have come a long way, and his products are on the road and in outer space.

The distance between what a professional is and what an amateur is has clearly shrunk in almost every industry. One of the drivers is access to the tools; another is access to the knowledge. What hasn't changed is the amount of passion and determination it takes to innovate. But success in a new start-up is no longer confined to the exclusive purview of the industry expert because access to knowledge, skill, and tools have been democratized over the last couple of decades.

CLUSTERED SYSTEMS

Let me introduce you to Phil Hughes and Bob Lipp. Phil and Bob were one of the early start-ups to rent space in our Menlo Park location. Electronic experts by training, both were semi-retired and in their late fifties or early sixties, well over the 29-year-old target age that VCs like to fund in the Valley.

Their idea was to use cooling liquid and a radiator system to cool server racks. Most racks at the time were designed to use just air-conditioning. The racks that were designed to use fluid were still very primitive.

Today, most of the cloud is built on huge warehouses stuffed with servers stacked on top of one another. The chips consume enormous amounts of electricity, and a stunning amount of electricity is used to run air-conditioning systems to keep those computers cool. In fact, computer centers consume 2 percent of all the energy in the United States and cost $250 billion in electricity a year globally (in 2010), a rate that is growing by double digits every year. It's a big business. IBM and Emerson Electronics are a couple of the Fortune 500 firms that compete in this space, providing cooling system solutions. A 10 percent improvement in cooling efficiency would mean $25 billion is saved electricity in a field that continues to grow by double digits each year.

Well, Phil and Bob were unable to raise money from venture capital firms in Silicon Valley, not too surprising when a $100,000 bet on some 29-year-old Stanford computer science student building applications for Facebook, Google, or the web could exit in a few years for hundreds of millions of dollars. Unless you were doing social, mobile, or gaming in the Valley in 2010, it wasn't easy to get VCs to invest in your project. Worse, if you were fiftysomething, working on something physical, and competing with IBM as a first-time entrepreneur, you were lucky to get a return phone call at all.

Consequently, Phil and Bob—the wrong ages and pursuing the wrong problem with major entrenched competitors—spent $20,000 of their own money and two years of their lives working on building a better mousetrap.

After they had built a fully functional prototype and were able to demonstrate it at a trade show, Sun Microsystems (now part of Oracle) and eBay expressed interest in supporting their efforts. Both Sun Microsystems and eBay were end users and fully understood the limitations of the current cooling systems. With further development and effort, Phil and Bob were able to land a multimillion-dollar Department of Energy (DOE) grant and build out and develop more systems. Eventually, because data centers were driving such demand for energy, the DOE held a "Global Chill-Off" where it invited all the large firms supplying equipment into this industry to a scientifically controlled and refereed competition—which Phil and Bob won. They beat IBM and Emerson. The folks at Emerson were smart enough to license the technology from Clustered Systems, Phil and Bob's company, and now sell it globally.

Note the most important piece of this development: the prototype.

In technology transfer circles, moving from concept to prototype is the underfunded valley of death. Prototypes can cost hundreds of thousands or millions of dollars. Or at least they used to. Not anymore. Teams can prototype their products themselves and save 95 percent of their development costs.

It was this realization that the game had changed for starting hardware companies that first drew me to TechShop. I met Phil and Bob in Menlo Park, and when they described what they were doing and how much they had spent, I couldn't believe my ears. Having worked at a couple of Fortune 500 manufacturing companies, I knew what it cost to develop prototypes. The molds alone, if done on the cheap, cost $15,000. Just scheduling a few focus groups took months of work and $20,000 to $50,000, and that was if you were only going to conduct a couple of local, cheap events. A national sampling could cost hundreds of thousands of dollars. And here were a couple of people building an entire system for under $20,000. And they weren't the only ones.

DIFFICULTY IS NOT A BARRIER

I like Phil and Bob's story because they, too, learned the skills they needed as they went along—welding, milling, CNC tooling, sandblasting, and powder coating. They designed, constructed, and built the entire cooling system themselves or, in a few instances, hired other makers to help them. Yet they were taking on players like IBM and Emerson Electronics in a field where they had no experience, and they were working on a very difficult problem. This is a mechanical, electronic, chemical, software, and computer problem. They had to manage a patent field with "picket fences" erected by engineering and legal departments from a few of the largest industrial companies in the world. Yet with two years of focused effort, learning, and failing fast, they succeeded. And this wasn't just a one-off improvement.

"The efficiency of the Clustered Systems' cooling system supports the greatest level of density and performance we've seen so far, and it has the legs to support several more product generations," according to Dr. Stephen Wheat, senior director of Intel High Performance Computing.[2]

JET PACK

I met Andy Filo soon after I started at TechShop in 2007. Andy had sold or licensed a number of toys to major toy companies over the years. He also consulted on design for the manufacturing process of high-volume manufacturing. Companies would hire him to help them scale up. But he was not working on a toy when I met him. Nope. He was working on a jet pack. Yep. A *jet pack*. Hello.

Early on, I asked him why.

His response? "Hey, GM, GE, and Boeing aren't working on it, and I was promised a jet pack. So if they won't work on it, I will."

And so Andy is working on a jet pack. Actually, he sells them. They only get about 30 seconds of flight time and use the "traditional" method of hydrogen peroxide to get enough thrust to get the pilot off the ground. But Andy has designed, built, and sold a jet pack to an event production company that uses it as a perennial crowd-pleaser.

Here is where it gets interesting. At TechShop, we conduct a lot of tours and presentations to large companies, educational institutions, and governmental agencies. We count each as a partner today and expect to develop many partnerships in the future. We had a large contingent of folks in from NASA at our San Jose location. After our PowerPoint presentation, there were still a few doubters in the crowd. Frankly, they scoffed at my slide of Andy's pilot flying around in a jet pack. However, as luck would have it, as we moved into the shop and the visitors started to wander around on their own, one of the NASA folks looked into Andy's workspace and saw a NASA jet pack on a stand in his suite.

"What's that?" he asked.

"A space pack from your agency." I said.

"What's it doing here?"

"I don't know. Let's ask Andy."

Andy came in and explained to them that as part of his due diligence he owned versions of all the jet packs ever made. He had just finished 3D printing a new nozzle that only a 3D printer could make and that could increase the thrust of the jets eight-fold. He then coyly asked, "You guys are doing this now, right?"

Nope.

Andy is now a contractor to NASA.

ORU KAYAK

I came in another time to the San Francisco location, and the staff told me I needed to meet Anton (Tony) Willis. He had taken over an entire table with a mound of corrugated plastic. It looked like some kind of folding plastic origami sci-fi film gone bad. I had no idea what he was working on.

"Hi, I'm Mark. What are you working on?"

"This," said Tony, spreading out his arms to visually encompass the plastic mess on the table, "is an origami kayak."

Silence.

Stunned silence.

"A what?"

"Well," Tony acknowledged, "I have some more work to do, but the basic idea has been laid out. I think it is going to work."

"An origami kayak?" I repeated. "Origami" and "kayak" are words I'd never heard in the same sentence before. Then again, the number of times I hear odd juxtapositions at TechShop—combinations of words, ideas, concepts that I've never heard anywhere else—is staggering. Things like, "This is a desktop diamond manufacturing device, a neutron shield for a fusion reactor, an engine design for a jet pack, a satellite, Mr. Potato Head for your head, a pterodactyl Flugtag flying device, "a fire tornado," "a lunar lander." But I digress.

"An origami kayak?" I asked again.

"Yes. You see, I love to kayak, and when I moved into my new apartment in downtown San Francisco, I no longer had room to store my kayak. I had also just read a book about origami and thought to myself, why not design a collapsible kayak?"

Hmm, I thought to myself. *Now there's an unfortunate turn of a phrase. I don't know anyone who would willingly buy a collapsible kayak.* Aloud, I said, "Interesting. How is it coming?"

"Oh, I have a long way to go yet, but I think it is going to work."

I watched Tony's progress over months of work with a combination of fascination and mild horror. A *collapsible* kayak? Tony made over 25 prototypes, took them out to the treacherous San Francisco Bay, and began to perfect the design. Eventually, he had test pilots with years of kayak experience try them out with very positive results.

"What's your next step?" I asked one day.

"I'm getting ready to launch a Kickstarter campaign to see if I can raise $80,000 and do a full production run."

"Seriously?!" I was surprised. "Eighty thousand dollars. That's a big campaign."

"Yes, but that is what I need. I launch the site tomorrow—can I include you in the e-mail blast about the launch?"

"Sure." I responded.

So the next morning, around 6 a.m., I received an e-mail announcing Tony's collapsible kayak campaign. I logged in shortly after 10 a.m. and saw he had already raised around $40,000. A very good start. Later that day, I was on call with a journalist who was asking me why I thought providing access to tools was so revolutionary. I asked her if she had heard of Kickstarter; she had. What would her response be, I asked, if a designer came to her investment group and asked it to invest in an origami kayak company? She replied that the group would, of course, take a pass.

"Exactly," I said. "Of course you would take a pass. Without a prototype or traction you would have to be crazy to do otherwise. But if the inventor could build a prototype and show it to a global audience of kayak people, he might be able to get it funded."

I went on to describe Tony's project and how it had just launched that morning. I asked the journalist to hang on while I checked his launch page to see how much money he had secured. The amount? Over $80,000. Tony had secured more than he needed to launch his company in a single day. The journalist wrote a nice article.

Tony finished the Kickstarter campaign with *$443,806* in funding. No angel group in the world would have provided that kind of funding under any kind of terms. It is a business that is unlikely to go public, have a billion-dollar exit, or secure a follow-on round. And now it is funded all through presales of products. Tony owns the company. He didn't have to give any of it away. That's $443,806 in sales.

DANNY

I met Danny Fukuba soon after I started at TechShop. He had just finished building an electric, self-balancing, 18-m.p.h. barstool, part of his project to build his own personal Segway since he couldn't afford to buy one. As the captain of a local robotics club, Danny had some basic skills. He then went online, found a mentor, and built his own Segway. Not bad. Gyros, aluminum welding, pc boards, circuits, and wiring, and he did it all himself.

Not too surprisingly, Danny was accepted by some top engineering schools in the country. Surprisingly, he didn't go. Instead, he began to teach himself everything he wanted to know by taking free classes online and build classes at our location in Menlo Park. While I do not recommend this career path to my children, we do need to recognize that going to college isn't for everyone. Actually, only 50 percent of high school graduates go to college, and a significant percentage of those who do go don't finish. Bill Gates, Mark Zuckerburg, and Steve Jobs all come to mind.

Eventually, Danny linked up with a friend, Sam Gordon, and they designed and created a beautiful smartphone stand made from of brushed aircraft aluminum. They, too, launched a Kickstarter campaign, looking for $10,000, and they raised $131,220.

Danny and Sam then worked with another TechShop member, Bradley Leong, on a stunningly gorgeous iPad keyboard design that basically turns an iPad into a MacBook Air "lite." They were looking for $90,000, a big number for a Kickstarter campaign, but they were trying to make a computer keyboard. That they could do it for $90,000, including their living expenses, is amazing. They raised $797,979.

In the few years since Danny graduated from high school, he has learned how to make just about anything and helped to design, develop, and sell almost a million dollars in products. I daresay he has had an amazing education. He also owns part of a company and is debt free. Maybe he will hire some of his peers from MIT once they graduate.

WHAT IS YOUR STORY?

It is a little early in this book to ask this, but I need to plant the seed.

What are you going to make?

We were born to make. If you were to enter a kindergarten class in your local school and ask the kids, "Who likes to make things?" every child would raise his or her hand. Everyone has ideas, though most stop fantasizing about them by the time they hit middle school. By then, they have learned that there is a single right answer to every question. That their art is either good and looks like the thing they are trying to draw, or not—and, therefore, they are not artists.

But the rules for success in the twenty-first century are emerging, and they are radically different from the rules in the nineteenth and twentieth centuries. You can make art, you can create, and you can sell those creations—or at least make them well enough that you or your loved ones would be thrilled to own the things you have made, be they chairs, desks, plates, cups, clothing, lamps, computer accessories, or whatever. If you are willing to climb the knowledge ladder needed, maybe you, too, could become the next Elon Musk, Jack Dorsey, Jim McKelvey, or even Jazz Tigan.

Here is the thing: You must learn to learn. We must learn to learn. We must develop our skills at creating, developing, and nurturing things and services that others value.

The age of being a cog in a big machine and marching one's way to a defined benefit plan retirement is over. In its place is a global talent pool with access to the same tools, knowledge, and equipment as everyone else and with competition coming from every angle inside and outside of the industry. Nokia and Motorola owned the cell phone industry top to bottom, and then BlackBerry came in to mess it up. But BlackBerry was just a harbinger of the change coming. Apple, at the time just a computer company, assaulted the cell phone cartel and won. It won big. And then Google—how crazy that is in retrospect—jumped in and changed it all up again. Now Samsung is making a good run at both of them.

I say just wait. As the operators figure out they need to open their systems up, all kinds of new competitors are likely to emerge from some pro-am's garage and take them on. I love the title of the former Intel CEO's book, *Only the Paranoid*

Survive. I would add, just because you're paranoid doesn't mean you will survive. Only those who learn will survive.

Just think about it. Elon takes on three industries and does well; Square takes on merchant banking and payment processing; Clustered Systems takes on IBM and Emerson and wins. These are very big wins. But Jazz is just as happy; you don't have to take on the world, change an industry, or have an enormous exit to live a better version of your life. You do have to try, learn, and improve. You do have to put yourself out there and risk failure. But in this new world, you don't have to go bankrupt if you fail because you can fail small. You can innovate as a hobby. Imagine that: a nation of innovation hobbyists working to make their lives more meaningful and the world a better place. Welcome to the maker revolution.

8

Distributed and Flexible Manufacturing

■ ■ ■

3D PRINTING

3D printing has become an overnight sensation—after 25 years. A couple of key patents expired and a bunch of small companies jumped in to create super cheap versions of what professionals have had for years.

For the uninitiated, this is a device, much like a printer, that can produce three-dimensional things out of plastic. The higher-end versions can actually do rubber or mixtures of different kinds of plastic. The highest-end versions use metal powder that is laser sintered (melted) into three-dimensional things.

The most common of the 3D printers, however, is simply a printer that extrudes a continuous stream of molten plastic that cools quickly to a hard plastic. This allows a computer controlling it to "print," or extrude, an object. They are fun to watch, easy to use, and very addictive. The price points are approaching consumer levels.

With the Internet at one's fingertips, it's possible to download ideas from sites like Thingiverse.com and start printing out toys and "jewelry" right away. Though it won't be possible to print out an iPhone anytime soon, it's easy to create fun and useful objects at home.

Jim Newton, TechShop's founder and chairman, went on a cross-country trip with his family recently. So that there would be more room in the family vehicle, Jim pulled out a center seat that was bolted to the floor. When he removed the bolts, he discovered that they went all the way through the floor. He now had the extra room he wanted but also got a lot of road noise coming through the holes in the floor. He could have reinserted the old bolts, but they would have stuck up too high and gotten in the way. He didn't want to cut the bolts down because after the trip he planned to put the seat back. So Jim measured the bolts, figured out how long they needed to be, determined what size of a bolt to use, and went on the McMaster-Carr website for a free download of the perfect bolt design he needed. (A number of websites provide files in a format that a 3D printer can print.) He then pulled the file into his design software, shortened the bolt to the length he wanted, adjusted the head to make it easier to use with his hands, and then printed the bolt out in ABS plastic on his home 3D printer. Just like that, he eliminated the ground noise.

Greg Gage enthralls audiences around the world by seem-ingly "hacking into a cockroach's nervous system" live and on stage. He does it to demonstrate how easy backyard science has become. His company, Backyard Brains, sells kits so kids can do the experiment themselves. Greg tells a compelling story about how, as a kid, he had learned it was possible to hook up special equipment to "listen" to a neuron fire in a brain and decided to pursue science so that one day he could do the experiment himself.

Well, life didn't turn out the way he was expecting. He studied hard in high school and thought that once he got to college in his major, he would get to play with this special equipment. Of course, that didn't happen. Greg had to study his major, take classes, and work in the labs he could get into, and he never got to work on the very expensive, specialized equipment. Only graduate students got to work in those labs. Greg went on to graduate school and eventually got his PhD in biomedical engineering, without ever having access to the tools to perform the "spike" test he had wanted to do since childhood. Then times changed. With sensors inexpensive and computers affordable, he built a small, simple, portable "spiker box" himself. And now he sells these boxes on the Internet for $99 dollars. Homegrown biomedical engineering experiments you can do at home. He'll even sell you a box of cockroaches.

Greg has gotten a lot of recognition for this nice little hack. He is now a TED Senior Fellow, has been named to CNN's The Next List, and has had numerous articles written about what he is doing. How this fits into TechShop: As part of the TED Fellows program, TechShop offers a free annual membership to all current TED Fellows. Greg is doing postdoc work at the University of Michigan, Ann Arbor, just 30 minutes away from the Dearborn location. He took advantage of our location in Dearborn outside of Detroit, and as a result, he has free access to sophisticated design software, 3D printers, laser cutters, and other tools. Backyard Brains has recently created a smartphone microscope that folds up neatly into a small handheld device that one can use with the phone's camera to do experiments.

Here is what is cool. Not only did Greg use the laser cutters and 3D printers to produce the prototypes, his company man-ufactures the devices on demand and uses the 3D printers and laser cutters for production. Manufacturing on demand. This is a pretty big deal.

We have been talking about using advanced manufacturing and personalization production methods for a long time. There are some decent-sized companies that do personalization through embellishment, such as adding a customer's name or an optional or custom design to the product. T-shirts, advertising specialties, laser etching, and so on are done this way. Very few companies actually manufacture an entire product on demand. But that is what Greg is doing. Backyard Brains makes a product after it is ordered, and the company uses advanced computer-controlled manufacturing systems to keep the costs low. Called "advanced manufacturing" in some circles, this approach is a revolution in manufacturing, and it is being driven by the reduced costs of these systems, tied with cheap computer systems and easy-to-learn-and-use software.

TYPES OF 3D PRINTERS

Three-dimensional printing was invented by Chuck Hall of 3D Systems in 1986 with the invention of a stereolithography (SLA) machine. This type of additive manufacturing uses an infrared laser to cure a polymer resin. The way it works is that there is a small containment vessel with a platform in the middle that can be lowered into the pool of polymer. The laser is computer controlled and fires at the pool, curing small sections of plastic while leaving the rest liquid. The platform then drops a little, the part drops just marginally below the surface of the liquid, and the laser fires again. In this way, a part is created out of the liquid polymer into a hard plastic.

These machines were very expensive, and the software was expensive and difficult to use. Only large companies, universities, and government research labs used them.

Fused deposition modeling (FDM) is the most common process we see now. Recently, the basic patents for the process expired, and an explosion of 3D printer companies have jumped in to design and produce them. An FDM machine is basically a very sophisticated glue gun. It uses a thin strand of plastic on a spool, feeds it into a heating head, and pushes, or extrudes, it out the head at a carefully calibrated speed. The head or platform then moves around, allowing one to build up a model one small globule of plastic at a time.

Leaders in this field include 3D Systems, Objet, and newcomers like MakerBot and Type A Machines. It's now possible to purchase one of these printers for around $1,200. With prices dropping every year, the machines are rapidly becoming a consumer product. These new price points have also made it practical to put a 3D printer on every designer desk, much like Ford recently announced it is going to do. This is brilliant. Giving rapid, low-cost, and easy prototype capability to designers can only help Ford designers do their jobs better, faster, and cheaper.

A second type of additive printer is the laser sintering platform. It operates the same way an SLA machine does in that there is a container of material (this time something solid), a platform, and a laser. The difference is that the material can be metal, ceramic, or a wide range of other types of materials. Jewelers have begun to use this system to create custom jewelry quickly on demand. Using computer processing, jewelers can also make incredibly intricate, complicated, and in some instances formerly impossible designs.

The ZPrinter uses an interesting hybrid approach. Like the SLA and laser sintering, there is a container with a material in it and a platform that drops as the material is hardened. Unlike the other two processes, however, this material is a powderlike substance that hardens when sprayed with a binder agent.

Using basic inkjet technology to control the head, the "inkjet" cartridge creates a nice platform that can actually operate in color.

Which of these printers one chooses to use depends on what one wants to accomplish. The ABS plastic you get from an FDM machine isn't as strong as an injection molded version, but it is strong enough for many applications. Boeing is famously using FDM machines in its production plants for the Dream Liner, producing various components on 3D printers. General Electric bought a 3D printing company for an undisclosed amount in early 2013 with the intent of increasing its use of 3D-printed parts in its jet engines. Watch for more of this kind of production to start happening globally.

These printers are kid magnets. Watching 3D printers in action is like watching fire. They are mesmerizing. Watching something emerge from nothing is magical. So magical, in fact, that a few years ago, as I was showing off a ZPrinter to kids at a Maker Faire, I started telling a few of them that the next year we would be printing puppies.

"Really?" they asked, their eyes getting real big, hoping I was telling them the truth and almost believing it because they were standing in front of a machine that was producing things right in front of their eyes.

I had to tell them no, we weren't going to be able to make puppies anytime soon, but that if they decided to become scientists maybe they could invent just such a machine when they got older.

In the scientific realm, researchers are experimenting with this technology, exploring how to use it to build kidneys, muscles, cartilage for ears, and more. Simple biological structures with a limited amount of cellular variety are well within reach.

HOME 3D PRINTER

I recently bought a 3D printer so I could better understand the current issues and opportunities surrounding them. It is an FDM printer fed by a cartridge filled with plastic filament that feeds into the print head. There is still work to do on software interoperability, and the quality constraints on the low end are still an issue. Still, it's already been a small hit in my household. After only about an hour, I had it set up, calibrated, and running its first "job." The device came with 15 basic designs, so I chose a linked bracelet. I ran the design through the modeling software that came with the machine to make sure that it would print, resized it just a little to make it larger, and then let it print.

The printer came with an obnoxious yellow-green color of plastic filament (I think it was my choice), but since our local high school sports green, it was a good choice. After some laughs about giving plastic jewelry to one's wife, mine accepted the first fruits of the printer and tried the yellow-green, plastic bracelet on. She immediately fell in love with its kookiness.

The next day, she decided to wear the bracelet to the school where she teaches, and it became the hit of the day.
"You mean you printed that out on a printer at home?"
"Does the printer cost $10,000?"
"How does it work?"
My wife is now a bona fide geek. When she explained to them the idea of printing things at home and how it only took 45 minutes, the kids were enthralled and the teachers impressed.

Following that success, I went online to Thingiverse .com, searched on "bow tie," and found some silly-looking

3D-printed ties. A file was available in the right format for free, so I downloaded it, ran it through the software, and printed out a yellow-green plastic bow tie. I'll never put it on, but I think my high school son is crazy enough to wear it on some spirit days.

Many inventions that we can't live without started out as hobbies and oddities. Cars, gramophones, telephones, and even bicycles were initially hobbies. Three-dimensional printing is too practical a tool to remain a hobby. Wait and see; many households will have them in the next 10 years.

MANUFACTURING IN A 3D WORLD

I am often asked why I would start a chain of makerspaces when it is clear we will someday be able to 3D print everything. This sentiment reminds me of discussions on the paperless office I had back in the early 1990s. The paperless office eventually led to having a printer on almost every desk and certainly in every computer-accessorized home in the world. It didn't reduce the number of printed things in the world even 20 years later. I'm pretty plugged in, yet I still get magazines, newspapers, annual reports, legal documents, and plenty else in printed form. I'm still dealing with as much or more paper as I ever have. So much new communication has occurred even as the percentage of things converted to paper has dropped,

Though the nature of 3D printing is disruptive and some things will certainly move to be printed at home or at work, I believe that the amount of "things" made by traditional means will continue to expand for a long, long time before 3D print technology will be able to replace them.

What do I mean?

Almost nothing I am wearing or sitting on will be seriously impacted by 3D printing in the next decade. Cotton is wonderfully made, and leather is very comfortable, durable, and useful. My watch is complex and beautiful (it was designed in 3D and prototyped with a 3D printer but manufactured traditionally). We have incredibly efficient, cheap, and high-quality goods produced by integrated supply chains and multinational competitors driving down the cost and improving the look and feel of everyday things. It is going to take a while for 3D printers to cost-effectively replace even day-to-day plastic items, much less than replace organic items like a silk dress.

There are likely to be some outliers. Recently, I saw a 3D-printed "fabric." It is basically plastic chain mail. Its "drape" is amazing; its "hand" is poor. I purposely just used two industry terms. The professional designer has the world at her fingertips and leverages every advantageous attribute to her advantage. Three-dimensional plastic and metal will have their attributes as well. Sometimes they will enhance, sometimes not; sometimes they will detract. Three-dimensional fabric will find its use—it may even be avant-garde for a while—but it isn't likely to replace cotton or silk any more than synthetics have replaced them.

When I was at Avery Dennison, we tested hundreds of different papers before settling on the one we launched for our ink-jet business cards. It needed the right hand, stiffness, brightness, edge bleed, and so on. We tracked 64 characteristics. If monochromatic ABS plastic were so wonderful, we would already be using it for everything. The fact that one doesn't make a living room sofa out of it today probably means we will not make a living room sofa out of it tomorrow, even if we could find a printer big enough, could wait the amount of time the sofa would take to "print," and were willing to spend the amount of money we would need to should we want it anyway.

3D printing is also trapped by geometric reality in that every time you double the size, you quadruple the price.

The most advanced printers today can do two or three types of extruded materials in multiple (read, not very many) colors. We are still experimenting with the idea of embedding wires, circuits, and other things into a 3D print process. Given current technological trends, most manufacturers don't have anything to worry about for a couple of decades. What they should do, though, is look for ways to take advantage of these printers to increase their capabilities, extend their supply chains, and improve their customer service.

This concern about *obsolescence* is driven by hype and a lack of understanding of how difficult the challenges are that face the new technology. I've been guilty myself. A close friend of mine bought a lead battery distribution company back in the early 1990s. I told him to be careful because electric cars were the future and that the vehicles would probably use lithium ion, not lead acid batteries. He was kind enough not to laugh at me. Electric cars are still the future, and their batteries will probably be made of lithium ion—and he will likely distribute those, too.

Last, making things is much, much harder than printing things. There are so many more variables involved. It is going to take something more disruptive than 3D printing in plastic to destroy manufacturing as we know it. More likely, 3D printing will just become more complex, more robust, and more roboticized. (More on that in a minute.)

No, 3D printing is not really about replacing things you can get already; it is really about things you want that aren't being made. Even Walmart can't carry everything. At the personal level, the reason you get a 3D printer will be about self-expression and making things that aren't made anywhere else.

3D-PRINTED GUNS—OH MY!

Only an idiot would 3D-print a gun. And only a poorly informed journalist with a bullhorn would think it was news. But it happened—well, sort of. I'm not a weapons expert, but I am a former Green Beret. The business ends of guns, the parts that matter most, are the barrel and upper receiver. These are made of steel. The barrel is made of steel milled out of a solid block. That way it will not blow up in your face and kill you. A hunting or military barrel is made with high alloy chrome molybdenum steel. The best barrels are made out of stainless steel. The pressure in a barrel when fired can exceed 50,000 psi; steel that can handle 100,000 psi is required to safely handle that pressure.

There may only be a handful of 3D printers in the world that can take powdered steel and make it that strong. The only reason one would use these tools would be to get at new geometries that can't be made any other way, or perhaps to improve the crystalline structure beyond what can be achieved in traditional smelting operations. These high-end metal laser-sintering 3D printers and manufacturing processes are so hard to do well that General Electric just decided to buy a company that specializes in the technology, Morris Technologies in Cincinnati. If printing a 3D weapon were so easy, why would GE need to buy a company to help with its aircraft engines?

Making a lower receiver (we need to watch our definitions here carefully: the lower receiver holds the bolt group, trigger, and magazine port) using a 3D printer can work, since technically it is really just the housing; however, even then it will not last very long. It requires machines that cost a lot of money, not your garden-variety home 3D printer, and it's still stupid. Making the trigger and bolt out of plastic would just be dumb. Even the famous Glock plastic pistol uses highly engineered plastic but uses steel for key components throughout the gun. You could 3D print a gun around a good barrel, bolt, and trigger group, and the like. But that is a far cry from 3D-printing a gun. Every gun I've ever seen came with a lower receiver. Why would someone print one? Guns are readily available in any black market in the world and most Walmarts. Printing a lower receiver and calling it 3D printing a gun is a cute PR device used to get some poor journalists who know nothing about guns self-righteously shaking their heads. I watched a couple of these sad folks shaking their heads, talking about something they had no experience with, never reaching out to anyone who knew anything about the topic. Just because it's on the Internet doesn't make it true, right? I did field a couple of calls from responsible journalists who then decided to ignore the story. Personally, I'm much more concerned about the security of the nuclear medical waste stream at *your* local hospital, but I'm off topic again.

Calling the lower receiver a gun is like 3D printing the doors of a vehicle and calling it a car. And that, too, would beg the question, why? The door would be of lower quality, very expensive, and slow to make. A 3D-printed receiver is of lower quality than a real one, more expensive, slower to make, *and dangerous.*

DARPA

The Defense Advanced Research Projects Agency (DARPA) famously developed the Internet. The agency spends billions of dollars on researching extraordinary ideas. If it isn't radical, crazy, or almost beyond the imagination, then DARPA is not interested. One of my recent favorites is a vaccine that reduces the amount of pain a soldier might feel with a catastrophic wound.

Another of my favorite DARPA projects is the Adaptive Vehicle Make program. This is an experiment in creating a new way to develop vehicle platforms for the military by crowdsourcing the design and then using a distributed manufacturing facility to build them. It actually worked. DARPA's first challenge was to help to create a military support vehicle, the XC2V. The design was crowdsourced and then built at an open platform vehicle production shop in Arizona called Local Motors. The winner of the design competition was awarded $7,500. Then Local Motors was paid to build the vehicle in its manufacturing facility. Fourteen weeks later it was done.

The program has been expanded into a multimillion-dollar effort to build a full combat vehicle. It is part of an advanced manufacturing effort where everything is fully digitized and then manufactured in a distributed manner. The basic idea is similar to why the Internet was built by DARPA: to be able to route communications through a network of connected computers with multiple redundant nodes spread out all over the United States and world. That way, if some nodes were destroyed, the communications system would be flexible enough to simply reroute communications around them.

Similarly, in a distributed manufacturing system, the destruction of a single plant wouldn't take down the entire manufacturing capability of a vehicle. It would be possible to "route around" the plant that had been destroyed and simply have another facility produce what was needed. In its eventual extreme implementation, industrial robots could be configured in a flexible manufacturing environment that would allow for rapid reconfiguration and autonomous manufacturing. We have a long way to go before that becomes a reality, and some of the challenges may be insurmountable with our current technology, but we will see some strong progress toward this idea over the next couple of decades.

The idea of flexible manufacturing is already being successfully deployed. Ford, unlike General Motors, decided that it couldn't forecast how many EcoBoost engines, hybrids, standard engines, or even diesel engines it would need, so it designed the car manufacturing line to be able to produce whatever was needed on demand. Ford just produces what is needed based on current demand. GM, on the other hand, built an entire production line devoted to the Volt electric vehicle. When demand did not develop, GM had to shut the plant down for a while to let inventory move through the sales channel. If the automaker could have developed a drive train with flexibility on an existing platform as Ford had done, it would not have found itself in the situation where it occasionally had to halt production.

KINKO'S FOR MANUFACTURING

It is not hard to imagine a future where flexible manufacturing capabilities are available like a FedEx Kinko's in every city in the United States and the world, stuffed with 3D printers, mills, lathes, robots, laser cutters, and people facile in making things, supervising robots as the robots make everything to order. You use the Internet to find that basic model of something you want, then find local sources for the materials, and change the design to meet your needs. Or mash it up with other basic models to make it uniquely yours and then "print" it to the local flexible manufacturing store.

There are plenty of serious obstacles in the way of making something like a smartphone at a facility like this, but simple products can already be made online at places like Shapeways .com.

At the time of this writing, there is a budding effort within the U.S. government to create a new advanced manufacturing research and development effort at up to 15 universities across the country. The idea is to seed the effort with $1 billion and convince universities and sponsoring private companies to bring another $1 billion to the effort. Focused areas in 3D printing, pharma, nano, and energy are envisioned.

An important part of the advanced manufacturing effort will be in the area of flexible automation systems. Though the focused domains may be from different disciplines and research areas, the basic tools that support the research will almost certainly be the same in most instances. As I've mentioned before, these include CNC tools, 3D printers, laser cutters, a plastics lab, an electronics lab, and even textiles.

It would be an absolute travesty if we spent that $2 billion and kept the communities out by making what is produced the exclusive purview of the university researchers and the research departments of sponsoring companies. The community doesn't need or want access to the full facility, but it would be easy to cordon off a public access lab from the specialized tools needed for the lab's other research.

ACCESS

It bears repeating that the real power of this envisioned open access facility is that it taps more deeply into the communities' capabilities and is nonexclusionary. The best innovations are driven by an individual's or team's personal passion and interest. Because labs and research facilities have always been closed off, I dare say most of the greatest innovations have not yet been developed. The raw capability of humanity has been constrained by an incredible lack of access.

Even within large companies, most of the creative individuals don't get to work on the new things. Think about it. If the typical spend at a large industrial company is 3 to 5 percent on research, then by definition most people are not working on innovation. That's fine; someone has to make the stuff that delivers the excess profits to fund research. But what this means is that most of the engineers in a large firm are working on today's products and are restricted to spending their energies on those products and those products only. Most engineers aren't in R&D and don't have access to those labs. And they likely work on activities around day-to-day production, and no general manager is ever going to let the engineers mess with innovation on a functioning production line (a quick way to get fired is to miss delivering on this quarter's sales quota because you are trying to innovate for something next year). Therefore, most (by far) of our highest trained engineering talent is not allowed to use that talent to innovate. And even if they do have 10 percent time or 20 percent time, they don't have access.

The largest industrial companies in the world *do not allow* most of their creative, experienced, and innovative engineers anywhere near a lab to innovate. They have them squirreled away on production and other activities. Many of these talented individuals end up in HR, finance, marketing, and sales. This is insane. Not that these creative people are in sales, but that they are in sales and their 10 percent time doesn't give them access to a lab. No. The world has changed, and it doesn't need to be this way anymore.

SELF-ASSEMBLY PROGRAMMABLE MATTER

The one real futuristic thing that would disrupt all this is molecular manufacturing programmable matter. Like the way the CNC machine was originally developed, the programable matter is being pursued by amazing scientists at MIT. I suspect they will get a bunch of DARPA funding. It would truly be revolutionary to be able to "program" materials to produce organic and nonorganic things. It sounds like science fiction, but then, so did going to the moon, or working underwater in submarines, or satellites, not that long ago.

I like the case for it. Think about it. Why not have a fast-growing maple tree that grows square, with no knots, and straight up with no limbs to get in the way? And if we could do that, why not have the tree curve so that a builder could plant two rows of them and have them grow into the framing for a house? Kill them in place, put in a subfloor and roof, and you have a home that was grown. OK, the square part's harder. But could scientists crack that genetic code? Maybe.

A step beyond that would be to harness the molecular manufacturing capability of bacteria and create things that can assemble themselves in a preprogrammed way. The research has started; however, practically speaking, consumer-grade usefulness is likely to still be at least 20 years away. And then, like many breakthroughs, it is likely that the products will have their own unique uses rather than simply replace that which came before. Because programmable matter would be by definition reprogrammable, it might be cheaper in the long run than manufactured goods. Though it might consume a lot of energy remaking itself, it still might actually be cheaper to use reprogrammable matter than organic matter.

I suspect that there might be intermediate steps like the one recently taken by Ginger Krieg Dosier, an assistant professor of architecture (repeat, *architecture*, not biological engineering) to reengineer bacteria to consume urea (yes, the stuff in pee), calcium chloride, and sand to make bricks.[1]

NASA is looking into this to see if Martian soil could be turned into bricks using water from the polar icecaps, astronaut pee, and bacteria. Yes, housing made of pee, dirt, and bacteria. Sign me up!

A GREAT TIME TO BE ALIVE

Is this a great time to be alive, or what? I firmly believe we are entering the greatest age of innovation and creativity in all of human history. They say we stand on the shoulders of giants. Yes, but we are standing on a hoard of giants now, and the tools, knowledge, markets, and financing have never been this easy to access. In economic-speak this is called "liquidity." Another way to look at it is "velocity."

A liquid market is one in which the ease of entering or exiting is low, simple, and fast. It is used to describe investment in publically held companies like Apple, Google, Ford, and GE—large companies with lots of people buying and selling the stock. Changes in the underlying value are quickly understood and reflected in the price. In a liquid market for innovation, the value of an idea would be quickly determined. One of the reasons that the Silicon Valley is the envy of the start-up world is that it has a stunningly efficient and liquid market of capital for start-ups—at least for start-ups focused on the last big thing.

Velocity is similar. It measures how fast money moves around in an economy. It is something of an odd concept but is very important for an economy. The idea goes something like this: On the first of the month, your employer pays you a dollar, which you then spend at a grocery store, which it uses to pay to its employees, who then spend it, and the cycle starts again. So, at the beginning of the month, you say you got $1, the grocery store says it got $1, and the employee got $1, so that $1 is actually $3. That is the basic idea behind velocity.

I believe skills development, knowledge distribution, and capture have a velocity component to them. When things that were formerly sophisticated and difficult to do become easier, it is like increasing the velocity of skill and knowledge. This has huge implications for the economy.

Now that the cost for a start-up, the access to knowledge, and the speed with which skills can be developed have all changed, I believe that the Silicon Valley is going to start losing its influence in the start-up landscape. It will not go away, but democratization, the low cost to try, and the liquidity of markets along with crowdfunding of the smallest start-ups is going to fundamentally change the game in the Silicon Valley.

This means it will be easier to start something great in the city where you are right now. Access to cheap, easy-to-use, and powerful tools along with access to market, funding, skills, and knowledge are completely revolutionizing the way things are created, developed, made, financed, sold, and even consumed. It is indeed a good time to be alive.

9

Accelerating Innovation

■ ■ ■

CORPORATIONS

I walked into my office in mid-2010 and found a note on my desk. "Bill from Ford called. He wants a TechShop. Call ASAP." My heart skipped a beat. "Bill from Ford."

Well, it wasn't Bill Ford, chairman and former CEO of Ford Motor Company (more on Bill Ford in a minute). It was Bill Coughlin, president of Ford Global Technology. Among Bill Coughlin's responsibilities as head of licensing at Ford is that of increasing the quality and number of patents Ford develops. He also happens to be a big believer in open innovation principles as a way of extending and expanding innovation coming into automobile companies. This may be considered radical by many in the industry, but Ford is doing some interesting things, like fully funding the development of a TechShop near its facilities in Dearborn, Michigan.

It took both organizations some time, but by the end of 2011, we had jointly opened a 40,000-square-foot open innovation center. And here is what happened next: Bill saw a 50 percent increase in the quantity of quality patent ideas flowing into his team.

What triggered this sudden increase in creativity? Bill bundled a TechShop membership into an award pool that Ford gives to employees who submit quality patent ideas. It is a noncash incentive, but it turned out to be a pretty big incentive.

The TechShop Detroit location has quickly become a feature of multiple press events hosted by Ford's PR and marketing. Literally hundreds of press people from around the globe come, hang out, make things, and see how Ford is pushing innovation out beyond the walls of its R&D organization.

It is one thing to keep sending "We Support Innovation" updates through the company newsletter, blog, and website. It is completely different to invest in and launch a physical embodiment of that commitment and to provide significant employee discounts for those who want to join it, or free memberships for those with quality patent ideas.

TechShop only takes up about half the Detroit–Allen Park facility, so Ford is moving groups from around Ford into offices and labs in other parts of the building. The first group to move in was the OpenXC platform team, another example of Ford embracing Open principles. Funded by Ford, this team is opening up automobile sensor data. Not just Ford's, but anyone's. The OpenXC team now has an open, extensible interface device that will allow anyone to grab data from Ford sensors and do new, innovative things with the data. Better, because it is an open platform, members in the OpenXC community are designing the OpenXC device to work with other car platforms. Ford is the first automobile company to open up this communications conduit, and this is emblematic of how forward its thinking is.

Ford started the OpenXC experiment a couple of years ago by letting some universities play with the sensor data being transmitted through a car. One of the teams created a Tweeting Ford Focus. Anytime the windshield wipers were turned on, a device tweeted the car's location and the fact that it was raining. It did a bunch of other cute things as well.

I want to play with OpenXC so I can track not just that my son may or may not be speeding, but also, by combining it with the accelerometer in his phone, be able to tell how fast he is accelerating and how many Gs he is pulling on a corner. Using this kind of tool, I'd know when he was doing doughnuts in the high school parking lot. Ford launched the OpenXC platform in January of 2013; anyone can now play with the sensor data coming out of any recently produced Ford.

Jim Newton and I did get to meet Bill Ford at the Computer History Museum in the Silicon Valley in 2012, where he told the audience, while answering the last question of the evening, that if Henry Ford were to start Ford Motor Company today, "He probably would have started in TechShop . . ."

UNIVERSITY CONNECTION

So, where are the universities in the scheme of this innovation revolution? Great question. A legal requirement for receiving some types of grants from the U.S. government is that the applying university or research institution must have a tech transfer office and effort. Ostensibly designed to provide patent and other commercialization support to researchers or to manage intellectual property (patents, inventions, software, or other copyrightable works) developed at the institution, a majority of technology transfer offices are famously inefficient. As an afterthought to the grant machines developed and designed to fund university research and professorial development, they do not drive any research objectives, have little power within a university, and are left to sell "technology" that was designed to help graduate students and professors get published and further their careers.

There is no market mechanism at play to help guide research policy. I don't know that there needs to be, I'm just pointing out the reality. As a result of this system, billions of research dollars are spent each year building great university engineering departments with little to show for it from an innovation perspective. The incentives are just not aligned. They still educate and then graduate students. It is their primary mission. Some universities also do some seriously hard research that isn't likely to be done in any other environment. This is not meant to be pejorative of the system, just a realistic view of the innovation results versus research and educational results.

Just as unfortunately, the university system is architected around domain fiefdoms. Consequently, schools of architecture, engineering, fine arts, and so on, rarely work closely together in a cross-disciplinary way. Designed to grant degrees to students who have demonstrated proficiency in their particular domains, each school is left to itself to scramble for grants, endowments, income, students, buildings, and infrastructure with help from the universities' administration.

Here is one of the results. Each major university department runs its own lab, often a small one, usually in the basement with limited access, limited hours, and supervised by graduate students part time. Many grants come with the need for machines, but often those machines are tied to that grant, not even the department. Operating the machinery in a safe, secure way is often an afterthought.

I recently visited a major university, which will remain anonymous, where I was told that, technically, if you were not in the department, the class, and doing domain-relevant research, you couldn't use any of the new machines attached to the grant. Makes sense, I guess. No point in creating liability, scheduling, or training problems unattached to the direct requirements of the grant. Furthermore, every department within this university was doing the same thing. Tens of millions of dollars' worth of equipment had been purchased within the last few years under this system. I learned this at a lunch that was pulled together by lab managers who had independently invited me to come and give a presentation. What was really funny about the meeting was that these four lab managers had never met before, had never been in one another's labs, and in a couple of instances, didn't even know the other school(s) had a lab. We had a great afternoon together taking tours of the labs, each of which had wildly different access, safety, hours, and operating assumptions.

ARIZONA STATE UNIVERSITY

Dr. Mitzi Montoya was on a panel with TechShop's founder, Jim Newton, when Jim described what a well-equipped makerspace entailed. As they say, "Timing is everything." Mitzi was in the process of building an innovation center in Chandler, Arizona, and wanted half of the 40,000 square feet dedicated to the machines her engineering students would need. As the vice provost and dean of the College of Technology and Innovation, Mitzi and her team were in the midst of figuring out what it needed to look like.

I'll paraphrase her response, but it went something like this:

"So, instead of a 20,000-square-foot space full of machines that are only available to our students, for a limited number of hours, supervised by other students, taught by other students, in an unaccountable, uncontrollable system . . . you could deliver an open access facility, professionally run, with safety protocols, insurance, and qualified instructors, that was open from 9 a.m. to midnight, and our students would interact with professionals from the community that probably work at Intel and General Dynamics. And we can layer in our innovation programs and attract other departments and schools with the ASU umbrella? We need to talk."

ASU will have the first university-sponsored open access DIY fabrication studio on the planet.

TOWARD A BETTER MODEL

Fabrication shops will become like libraries, medical clinics, and gymnasiums at universities. They will be central resources to be used by the entire school and, like the medical clinics, the entire community. Regional high-tech manufacturing centers will be colocated within the university structure but off-site, leveraging the billions of dollars in research grants, tied in with the technology transfer office and local incubator infrastructure.

This will help drive innovation in a cross-disciplinary, open access, leveraged way. No longer will the architecture department have "all the laser cutters," the art department "all the woodworking machines," and the mechanical engineering school "all the metal machines." No longer will high school kids have to wait until college to have access to equipment, and no longer will local artists, engineers, or entrepreneurs have to mortgage their homes to get the machines they need in order to produce while the very machines they need sit idle most of the time at their local university. For a small fee, they will have them right in their own communities.

We have already started to explore this model with Arizona State University and the Technical University of Munich in Germany. The general idea is to provide access to students who need a prototyping lab for their studies, get companies in the local community to help support it, and supplement overhead support requirements by opening up the platform to anyone in the community who is willing to pay.

STANFORD D.SCHOOL

There are a couple of schools that are closer to what I'm proposing—MIT's Center for Bits to Atoms and Stanford's Hasso Plattner Institute of Design or d.school. We have a location close to Stanford University and have had a number of projects come out of the d.school. Interestingly enough, the d.school isn't actually a school within Stanford; it is a series of integrative classes that can be taken by anyone in a graduate program at Stanford. D.school is integrative in that it takes the expertise created in other degree granting programs, combines the students, and creates challenging real-world projects. It also has a lab space with many of the same tools that a great makerspace would have.

EMBRACE

I covered the Embrace baby warmer in an earlier chapter, but I want to make sure the handoff between d.school and TechShop is clear. At the end of the semester, Jane Chen's d.school team had successfully developed and demonstrated an infant warming blanket that could be used as poor communities' version of an incubator or as a transportation device that would ensure a child a life-saving few more hours of regulated temperature in the blanket while being transported to an incubator. Then the design class ended. The baby warmer that was to become Embrace was not funded by a research grant; it was a class project. There are no labs at Stanford designed to support commercialization of projects that have been completed. Where was it supposed to go? The team members got their grades, many completed their degrees, and their time at Stanford came to an end. The prototype, however, needed more work if anything was to become of it. That is where our open access shop came in. Without a hiccup, the team of Stanford students moved development to TechShop and kept going. It was cheap enough that they were able to then go out and find grants to create their nonprofit. Since then they have fully developed the blanket, launched in multiple countries around the world, and the warmer has saved 5,000 babies so far.

But note: the university was not architected to support or sponsor the ensuing company. Furthermore, and understandably, the d.school lab is not open to the community. It is outside the current mission of university labs to be community resources. That has got to change.

SOLUM

Solum has a similar story. The company grew out of a Stanford class, in this case, the MS&E 273 Technology Venture Formation course. Nick Koshnick, Justin White, Mike Preiner, and John Paul Strachan formed a team to tackle the problem farmers have of determining how much fertilizer to lay down for any given season's crops. This is a huge issue for farmers. Too little fertilizer, and the planned crop yield drops, potentially causing the enterprise to fail. Too much fertilizer, and the crop yield might be favorable, but it is very expensive. In addition, overfertilizing can result in burning and killing the plants. It is, for example, a primary contributor to the large dead zone the United States has at the end of the Mississippi River. Nick and his team set out to solve these problems. Nick had taken Stanford's Technology Venture Formation course, designed to help graduating students develop businesses, and he had just received a PhD from the university, so in essence, Stanford launched Nick's team. But the team didn't have access to a lab.

That is how I learned about it. I had seen Nick and his team out in the shop working on their first prototype, which had led to a very small investment round whereupon they moved into the office next to mine. Within months, the team had developed multiple prototypes, hired a half a dozen employees, and started to burst out of the little office where they were working. Very quickly, at least by product development standards, they had gone through a series of prototypes, attracted more talent, and raised around $2 million in their Series A, at which time they graduated and moved out.

Since then, the company has raised about $20 million total from some of Silicon Valley's top firms and has become a very exciting, award-winning agricultural start-up.

One the keys to Solum's fast launch was access to a platform that could support its development. There was no stage-gated process, no incubator boot camp, and no business plan competition. Again, the key was in building the prototypes—that is what got them launched. The remarkable speed with which Solum was able to go through each prototype was driven by *direct access to the tools*. The team could develop a product and test, develop again, and test again. There was no need to ship drawings and test rigs all over the world. There were no off-site meetings to schedule with design consultants. This was built with speed.

Once again, there was no real involvement from the university. Nor does Stanford have any claim in the company. Had the team done its research, design, and company launch on a campus at almost any other university in the United States, the university would have claimed intellectual property rights and wanted licensing fees. Graduate students at many universities don't own their IPs; the university does. This strikes me as an odd arrangement. Sure, if you are working on a grant funded by the university and being paid by the university for that research. But why should the university own something outside the area of research? And why is the licensing so hard?

This is normal, by the way, for most big companies as well. Employment agreements state that the business owns its employees' ideas, whether they were developed on company time or equipment or not. Since access to tools has been fairly limited over the years, this arrangement hasn't been fought very much. As access to tools becomes ubiquitous, however, I suspect companies are going to get more pushback from their employees.

In the preceding examples, Stanford University had a significant part to play in the overall ecosystem of helping to develop these start-ups, but the university wasn't part of the launch. These start-ups did not come out of the university's tech transfer office; there were no government or foundation grants supporting them. They just launched the companies themselves because they could.

DRIPTECH

This start-up is similar to Embrace in that it started as a class project at Stanford's d.school. TechShop didn't have a lot of engagement with the team, but one of its lead engineers, Trevor

Boswell, used our site for some of the early development of a key machine. Driptech was started by Peter Frykman after visiting Ethiopia as part of Stanford's Entrepreneurial Design for Extreme Affordability class. He saw firsthand how difficult irrigation was for small plot farmers and developed a super-low-cost drip irrigation system for them. Driptech has won various awards, including one from the World Economic Forum.

COMMUNITY RESOURCE

A senior executive told me recently that his organization had more engineers working outside of R&D than it did in R&D, and that, in fact, given the company's preference for hiring engineering talent and then cross-training the talent in other disciplines, it had plenty of engineers in its HR, finance, and marketing departments.

I pointed out that one didn't have to be an engineer anymore to design, develop, and launch a product. The senior executive conceded that, but said it was off point. His concern was that literally none of the engineers in the company, including those in research and development, could pursue areas of research that could help the company innovate outside of those areas of research that were already approved, and that many of the talented engineers were no longer anywhere near R&D. In a sense, many of them were closer to the market in marketing and sales than the R&D team was. In theory, marketing and sales have input into the priorities inside a company, but certainly not always. So how does one solve the dilemma that great minds, insights, and ideas were not being developed?

This executive was advocating a makerspace membership as a way of opening up internal creativity. I could not agree more heartily. But if you want to have an even bigger impact, you should open the space up to the entire community, universities in town, other manufacturers, high schools, elementary schools, start-ups, and other small-to-medium-sized enterprises (SMEs). And then if you really wanted to take it to the next level, you would wrap it into a national and global network of these spaces.

Why would one want to reduce the diversity, knowledge, and skills available? One answer: intellectual property (IP). But this is a false choice; it is not an either-or situation. Yes, IP is important, but if you use it to isolate yourself, you will be outpaced by those who have figured out how to be more open and yet compete on IP where it matters, protected in open environments through cloaking or other mechanisms, including a locked private area of one's own. It is not an either-or; it is just another IP situation to manage. IP is already being managed; it can also be managed in environments like a makerspace. Furthermore, I have yet to hear of anyone stealing IP in our makerspaces, while I always hear people say the community has added IP and given it to them—sometimes in patentable ways.

So in an attempt to protect its IP in what I would describe as Neanderthal ways, a firm puts itself at risk to be outpaced by firms that have figured out how to deal with open innovation and makerspaces.

TAKE IT UP A LEVEL

A fab lab is usually around 2,000 square feet or so. A typical hackerspace can get as big as 4,000 square feet and sometimes larger. A well-equipped makerspace starts at around 13,000 square feet, and a couple of our joint projects with Ford and ASU will run around 40,000 square feet in size when offices and classrooms are included. But what would happen if we took the 5M Project model and scaled up to an innovation hub? This would approach more of the size of an industrial sector play, where 250,000 to 1,000,000 square feet with mixed-use property would be developed in or near city centers, redevelopment zones, and universities.

The largest and most active true office-based incubators that offer start-up through midsized office space approach the 200,000-square-foot size. The advanced manufacturing platforms envisioned by the Department of Commerce run from 50,000 to 100,000 square feet exclusive of office support, retail, apartments, or restaurants. Combine that with university research or large biotech or nanotech incubators (which tend to be very expensive and large), and one could easily see 1 million square feet of mixed-use development. The economic benefit, educational support, community development, and industry support would be enormous.

Examples of this size of development are spread out around the world. The key difference here is in imbedding the open access component; this changes the nature and dynamic of the complex in a very powerful way. There is a big opportunity for those existing facilities, to begin retrofitting them with FabLabs, hackerspaces, and makerspaces.

The power of the open space is that students, professors, and university lab researchers would now have opportunities to mingle with commercial enterprise engineers, local artists, and entrepreneurs. Essentially, these open spaces become the innovation commons where anyone can come and work.

There is a role for the state and foundations as well. Funding for makerspaces is still scarce and provided mostly by the well-endowed universities, corporations, and middle-class makers. Apart from the occasional fab lab in a school setting, communities that are underprivileged, poor, disenfranchised, or marginalized cannot yet afford this kind of offering. I believe this needs to be fixed. Unfortunately, there are real hardware costs, real estate, utilities, and payrolls associated with fab labs, hackerspaces, and makerspaces—unlike software, where you can just duplicate it, create a school support channel or start-up support channel, and give the software away at no marginal cost. Whether through subsidies, scholarships, field trips, grants, or training programs, the Maker Movement needs to find a way to become more socioeconomically inclusive.

FOUNDATIONS

The Maker Movement needs some help from foundations. Early on, it was pointed out to me that state educational institutions are not really designed to experiment—at least not in the true sense of the word. They need proof points from somewhere in order to be able to justify an expense. Foundations, on the other hand, help fund experiments, and they create metrics (sometimes new metrics) to track and validate the usefulness of an innovation. There is plenty of anecdotal evidence that exposure to hands-on learning and tools can help motivate a child to consider science, technology, engineering, or math as a career. My favorite recent example happened with a partner of ours at South by Southwest (SXSW), an annual music, film, and interactive conference and festival in Austin, Texas, in 2012.

General Electric had created a traveling road show, GE Garages powered by TechShop, in 2012. One of the first stops was at SXSW. We had MakerBots (3D printers), Inventables (remarkable materials), and TechShop employees spread out around the site running laser cutters, welding machines, CNC routers, 3D printers, hand tools, and other tools for people to use.

That first Saturday, a 14-year-old girl stumbled onto the five containers of advanced manufacturing equipment on the corner where we had set up, and she brought her father over to see what was going on. Little did he know, Dad had just lost most of his weekend at SXSW to our site. The girl spent four hours on-site that Saturday, learned all about the tools, met our staff, hung out with other makers, and learned how to tack weld.

Yes, you heard me right. As part of the project, we had teamed up with GE to give away bicycle racks that were being welded as part of the demonstration. Observers were given short instructions on how to tack weld and then sent to a station where they were able to help weld together the bicycle racks. This girl was very excited about what she had learned and came back the second day to start welding a bike rack for her school. Then the unexpected happened.

A group of senior marketing folks from GE came by to see how the installation was working. I have to give them credit, this was an installation like none I've ever seen; working the logistics to get this equipment set up, staff trained, and the space opened up to the public in a safe, controlled way was very impressive. But before the GE folks approved the next locations, they wanted to see this one in action.

When our newfound friend found out the sponsors were on-site, she insisted on meeting them and proceeded to thank them for giving her the chance to weld a bike rack for her school even though she had never welded before. She told them the installation had changed her life. Based on the experience she had had that weekend, she had decided that she was going to become an engineer.

What a great opportunity. Currently, only 10 percent of American women pursue engineering as a viable employment option—even during the greatest explosion of materials knowledge creation and easy-to-use, powerful, and cheap tools. Capturing the talent and creativity of half the world's population by encouraging this group to consider STEM careers (science, technology, engineering, and mathematics) is one of the biggest opportunities we have in the world. And we have to get to kids when they are young and still deciding what they are "good at" and "not good at"—14 years old is generally too late.

What pathways work in getting them excited is a core question, and state-run institutions don't have the funding or bandwidth to drive this type of experimentation. Some do, and some will try, but this is the very function of foundations and other charitable organizations: to blaze new paths for others to follow.

We are still early on in this movement, so I'm very confident all these things will come, but it takes individuals in the right place and at the right time to make them happen. It takes vision, risk acceptance, and funding to make a real dent in the universe. It is going to take the entire community to leverage the emergent opportunity that the Maker Movement is enabling.

MAKERSPACE AS CATALYST

Access to tools is so fundamental to economic development, learning, start-ups, artists, research, and production that I can see it driving the development of entire communities. Much like how a university town can grow into a city, so could the well-placed development of tools, training, and access grow a vibrant creative cluster in a city. As a way to differentiate a city, county or region, the development of open access facilities in conjunction with schools, vocational training, and commerce will be huge. Already, people have moved to the

Bay Area to be near our space. Yes, moved. As in relocated themselves and their belongings.

At TechShop, we see people start companies that couldn't get started any other way. First robotics teams come in and use our space, further cementing the career track these kids are interested in. Tools and infrastructure will become a key differentiator for some people in choosing where they want to live. Knowledge now flows through the Internet; coding, calculus, and chemistry can be taught and learned at any high school or university; but access to a CNC waterjet for all comers is not available on the Internet. Eventually it will be in some form, but it will be more expensive than operating it yourself. So right now, there are first-mover advantages to be had for the cities that develop these spaces and attract the talent to use them. True, because building these spaces is hard, physical, and requires more than just desks and heat, there will be a slow build out. However, this trend, the third industrial revolution or hardware 2.0, the Maker Movement revolution, or whatever you want to call it, is going to be bigger than the web. With the explosion of mobile, social, and gaming incubators being spun up around universities across the world, it will be easy to leverage that energy and infrastructure into a hardware renaissance—once the tools are available.

Changing through
Participation

■　■　■

I n this chapter, I'm going to talk about how to get engaged
with the Maker Movement. There are plenty of ways, and
I'll hit a number of them in the following pages. The point is
simple. Make something, anything.

MEDIA FUN

I had a friend who worked for a fitness magazine. He told me
that 80 percent of the readers didn't work out. I was stunned. I
know that many might not be working out, but 80 percent? He
said being fit was more like football, a spectator sport. People
liked the content, liked to learn and imagine how they might
work out, and even liked to plan how they were going to work
out. They just never get around to it. To illustrate his point, he

told me how one day when he was at a garage sale, he spied some very early weight lifting dumbbells in the man's garage. My friend likes to collect early versions of workout gear, so he went over to inspect the weights, which were from the early 1960s. It was pretty rare stuff.

He asked the 70-year-old owner if they were for sale. "Oh, no, I've been meaning to start using those," replied the man. "I'll probably start next week." They were still in the original box. This man was going to get started "next week" for decades.

I learned a couple of things from this. First, just because everyone who reads a magazine is not a participant doesn't mean there aren't a lot of participants. They just consume the hobby in a different way. But because they are supporting the movement through reading about it and buying the occasional kit or package (used or not), they help support the overall movement. Second, the level of passion and belief about the value of the movement goes very deep. That owner would never sell those weights. The fitness lifestyle consumer, even if he didn't work out, still believed that any day now, even after decades of not working out, he was about to start working out. What is nice here, though, is that even in his delusional belief that he was going to start lifting any day he helped perpetuate the movement through his belief in the movement.

Make: magazine was modeled after the old *Popular Mechanics* magazine. The idea was that there used to be a lot of instructions on how to actually make things in *Popular Mechanics*. I love both magazines. There's an entire television channel dedicated to do-it-yourself projects, and shows like *Mythbusters*, *Monster Garage*, various build shows, and even *Iron Chef* or The Food Channel are all about making things. But just because you watch *Iron Chef* doesn't mean you are a great cook. You might be one day, you may plan to be one day, but for now you enjoy it vicariously.

There are a range of reasons that people read, watch, and learn, but don't do. I'm thankful for them because they encourage the basic informational providers to keep publishing. But for a movement to really sustain itself, it has to have doers.

STEM

Science, technology, engineering, and math classes, or STEM as they are known within the educational community, have become a rallying cry. It makes a lot of sense. If we (this is the global we) can get more people working in these fields, the world is more likely to innovate its way out of many of its current most pressing technical challenges. The key, though, to getting kids excited is to engage them in hands-on activities with the age-appropriate technology.

I'm a big believer in the First Robotics program, LEGO's robot program, and the F1 Racing build program where kids get to make models of race cars and then race them with radio controls. These programs are fun, educational, and addictive. They do require funds for the equipment, space, and training facilities. It is unfortunate that most schools lack the resources to fund these types of activities. Perhaps a central resource within a community could be utilized though that creates significant transportation issues.

MINI MAKER FAIRES

Maker Faire has a nice streamlined process for authorizing local mini-Maker Faires. A typical Mini Maker Faire will have 50 to 100 maker booths, with the usual eclectic variety of people, projects, and products seen at a full-sized Maker Faire. Along with the quilts, jewelry, paintings, and arts and handicrafts that are staples of traditional art fairs, one will find booths spilling over with robots, chemistry sets, physics toys, steam punk outfits and devices, robots, 3D printers, and electronics. These events are particularly family friendly and unleash children's imaginations. They make for a great weekend. If there isn't one in your city, organize one.

BRIGHTWORKS

Gever Tulley is an inspiration. At a TED talk in Monterey, California, a few years ago, he introduced the core of his book in progress. "Five Dangerous Things You Should Let Your Kids Do" was an excerpt from his book *50 Dangerous Things (You Should Let Your Children Do)*. With a nod to safety, he proceeded to tell the audience that they should let their children play with fire, own a pocketknife, and do other dangerous things.[1] Not too surprisingly, no publisher would touch it. So he self-published, and it became a global bestseller. It helped that one country tried to ban the book. I mentioned his camps earlier where the design principle was to make sure there was a reasonable chance of the build being a failure.

He tells a story of one of the first camps where the group was building a small roller coaster and the design was given over to the kid who could draw the best. The young kid then drew a fanciful roller coaster with a jump over a pit of fire. Gever couldn't get the child to give up on the pit of fire jump until he pointed out that not only might it not work well, but the child's mother might fall into it. Reluctantly, the child relented. And they eventually got a small backyard roller coaster working.

Gever has gone on to create a school, Brightworks, that incorporates some of the best current thinking around project-based, cross-disciplinary education. I highly recommend finding local schools that are looking to incorporate this kind of instruction into their offerings or have project-based learning as a core principle. If there isn't one in your community, maybe it's time to start one.

MAKE SOMETHING

One of the ways to get hooked on making is to build or construct something and give it to a friend or family member. If thought goes into the item beforehand and it is crafted with a specific person in mind, there is almost no greater feeling than giving away something you have made. At some of the events where I'm asked to speak, I talk about "radicalizing" an audience. Not in a political way, but in a personal way. I cover some of the material in this book and then challenge the audience to participate in the revolution simply by making something for a loved one. I then tell them that after they have given that something away, they need to reflect on how they feel about the process and themselves and the gift after they have given it away. Making a gift is profoundly different from running down to the store and buying something for someone. This act is part of how one radicalizes another person. Get the person to do something explicitly in support of a revolution and do it with deep emotional and personal value. The gift-giving trick is very powerful, transformational, and life changing.

Here's the thing: The gift doesn't have to be designed or made from scratch in order to be emotionally significant to either the giver or the receiver. Simply modifying or having input into a design can make the design yours.

Years ago, I led a team that put interactive multimedia printing kiosks into Walmart and Staples. These machines were amazing. Using a laser printer and an advanced printing cabinet, one could make business cards, letterhead, certificates, postcards, and labels instantly. We hired some world-class designers to help us create the best designs; we had a software intelligence program that would not allow one to make a bad-looking card or letterhead. All the user had to do was enter the relevant information onto a form at the start and begin making selections. The program would refine and develop a business card. At the end, a custom card would be printed out. It was a nice system.

One of the big surprises for me came when we interviewed people about their purchases. First, they were paying as much as 20 cents per business card when they could have gone to a printer and gotten 500 for $19.95 or less. But most important, the purchasers would tell us that they loved the fact that they got to design the card. They would hold it up and with pride of ownership say, "Look what I made."

This floored me, for the customers didn't design the business card; we did. They didn't make it look good; we designed the system so they couldn't make their product look bad. Yet because they input their address and name, selected a font (from a carefully restricted set of fonts) and design (that we had chosen to match the font and other elements on the card), customers felt they had designed their cards. You don't have to grow the tree, cut the timber, plane and mill it, and then lathe and sand it to feel like you "made" a picture frame. No. Even if all you do is embellish it with paint or etch it with a laser cutter, you can say with pride, "Look what I made."

Recently, this was driven home for me again. At TechShop, we host many corporate events. One of them provides participants with the opportunity to use the plasma cutter (a machine that uses electricity and air to create a plasma knife that cuts through steel) to cut out their company logo. The group then gets to weld it, under careful watch of one of our Dream Consultants. For this particular event, 30 executives were coming, so we precut 28 company logos to help speed up the process.

The plasma cutter is fun; it cuts steel like butter, melting away the steel quickly. The evening of the event, in front of all the executives, a Dream Consultant loaded the logo into the computer program, hit the button to start the cut, and 20 to 30 seconds later the cut piece was ready to be dropped into a bucket of water for cooling. A big billow of steam came out with a nice sizzle from the water boiling instantly when it touched the hot steel. The Dream Consultant demonstrated the process twice to show the executives how the process worked and then started to distribute the precut steel. The executives would have none of it. They wanted to "make it themselves."

I almost laughed. We grabbed the design, scaled it, prepared it, and set up the machine code and machine. All that was left for the participants to do was to hit the "start" button on the computer screen, pick up the piece with a pair of tongs at the end of the job, and plunge it into the water. But the group members still felt like they had "made" their industrial logo art because they got to hit the "start" button. The event ended up running 30 minutes overtime just so everyone could stand around watching one another "make" the company logo.

All this is to say, you can start on your own road to becoming a maker just by modifying existing things to add your piece of effort, design, or panache. It lowers the hurdle while delivering much of the physiological benefit. Start small and build.

SOFTWARE

Play with software. I'm a big fan of Autodesk, whose senior management team is made up of makers. Autodesk has gotten serious about consumer software and making it easier to design. The consumer software now includes a free 3D scanner application that can be used with a smartphone, and a great "creature" making software that allows one to create creatures on an iPad. It is easy enough to use that an eight-year-old can do it.

Just as my generation had to learn how to use Microsoft Word, PowerPoint, and Excel, if not HTML, the next generation will become fluent in polygons and 3D printing. It's easy to get started with some great free or low-cost design packages, many from Autodesk. With the basic software and access to the libraries of predesigned things on the Autodesk website, on Thingiverse.com, or in unlikely places like McMasterCarr.com, you can participate in the next revolution.

3D PRINTER

I talked at length about 3D printers earlier, but I want to come back in this chapter and drive the point home. Though 3D printers have a limited range of capabilities, they are wonderful tools for creating prototypes and toys, and they have great educational value. For the play value, toys, and prototypes you can make in your home, I strongly suggest you invest in one of these amazing machines or get access to one somehow. They are just too much fun. When combined with easy-to-use software, you will be able to work with your young children, create a design together, and print it out today. I suspect a 3D printer will become the breakout hit of a Christmas season sometime soon. And 30 years from now, your children will remember being introduced to the future through your giving them access to just such a machine.

GROW SOMETHING

Let's not forget biology. First, planting and growing is a form of making. With less than 3 percent of people in the United States employed as farmers, we forget this. A great deal of satisfaction is to be had in having a garden out back where you grow some of your own food. It can be a lot of fun and great family time. The food is usually better for you, tastier, and can also be cheaper than store-bought produce.

Or start a biolab in your community. Check out diybio.org to find a lab near where you live. I found Genspace in Brooklyn while scouting for a location there. Up on the seventh floor of an old bank building is the first level-one safety, open access, DIY biolab in the United States. As I got the tour, my guide let me know that Genspace had contacted Homeland Security ahead of time to let the agency know what it was doing. Genspace also pulled together an advisory board to oversee safety, only allows work on biologics that are harmless, and has an amazing group of founders and members. There aren't many of these labs now in the United States or around the world, but because the costs to get started are low for entry-level exploration, I expect to see many more. If you have a biotech firm in the area, it should be sponsoring its own Genspace equivalent as a community outreach effort.

MAKER VACATION

Take a maker vacation and book some learning time at a makerspace. A number of people take short, weekend, or even extended vacations hanging out in San Francisco and plugging into our space. A few have come for a month or even two.

They schedule a ton of classes at the start of the month right as the class list is posted and start taking classes back-to-back-to-back. It is a great way to get plugged into the local maker community. These folks meet a bunch of other students, most of the instructors, and since they are around for a day, week, or month, they get to know the staff. They become part of the fabric of the community quickly, learning as they go, joining other projects and creating their own, bringing in family members and friends throughout the month as people in their lives come visit them on vacation. It is an amazing way to jump into the maker scene.

Another vacation option is to organize it around a Mini Maker Faire, or maybe even one of the bigger ones. I know plenty of people who take a long weekend to enjoy the Maker Faire as much as they can. The Bay Area and New York Maker Faires along with the U.K. Maker Faire take place every year.

MOVE

Most of us don't have the flexibility to jump in this deeply, but a number of people have relocated to be close to our shops.

When I was at SXSW in Austin, Texas, this year, I met someone who did this. This former Microsoft employee from Seattle had been waiting for us to open a location in a city with a lower cost of living in the South. Within a few months of our opening in Round Rock, Texas, 20 minutes north of Austin, the man moved out of Seattle and into Austin. What was really interesting with him was that unlike the others I know who have moved to be closer to our makerspace, he did it for general reasons—he simply wanted to be close to a shop. All the others I've met had some kind of specific business-related project they needed to get done. I've met people who moved from a low-cost area like Phoenix, Arizona, to the Bay Area because the project they needed to complete couldn't be done any other way. Access to tools is a great motivator.

JUST DO IT

Find a project that you can work on where you have the tools you need already. Lowe's has an entire selection of projects, as does Instructables.com and other websites. You never know what might happen. Remember Tina Lax from earlier? She committed herself to make something and ended up running a business. David Lang started by writing a blog, "Zero to Maker," and now owns a robot company.

I met a man a couple of weeks ago who had dreadlocks down to his knees, shredded jeans, and a leather jacket with amazing etchings all over it. I went over to see what he was working on and discovered another accidental entrepreneur. He was making leather dog collars using the laser cutter. He said he had made himself a leather choker with all kinds of etchings and studs on it, and one of his acquaintances wanted one like it for his dog. Then a local pet store wanted some, and then so did another, and now he was supplementing his living making leather dog collars, after taking just one class. Yes, one class. Sixty dollars for the class and less than three hours of instruction.

Another new friend is a semiretired software exec who just wanted to learn how to make things. Within a few weeks, he was making all kinds of things for his child's school: laser-cut invitations for an event coming up, stage props for the school play. Then an arbor for a garden project and an elaborate CNC-cut entryway for a fund-raising gala. Most recently, he signed on with some other members to launch a start-up.

LITTLEBITS, ADAFRUIT, AND ARDUINO

If you don't have access to much in the way of a makerspace, I would recommend getting started with a transitional technology. Some ideas? Building a drone, buying some electronics projects, or working with the little folks in your life with littleBits.

A project that came out the MIT Media Lab, littleBits is like little LEGOs that snap together using magnets in an array of sequences that allow children of all ages to explore the fun of assembling electronics without having to solder and understand much of anything. It really is like LEGOs for electronics. A small kit will let you make a buzzer, a light, or other thing and hook up sensors to it. Press on the pressure pad, and it lights up. Put in a motion sensor and wave at it. With dozens of other ways to interact with the pieces, they are a lot of fun.

Adafruit and SparkFun have a wide array of projects, beginning with ones that are a step up from littleBits and all the way up to robots. They are a great resource for electronic fun, including electronic fashion accessories. There is something here for everyone. Both are big supporters of the Arduino open source controller hardware.

The next step up, complexity-wise, is Arduino. A microcontroller that helps to bridge electronics and computers into the real world through sensors, motors, and other devices, it is a very powerful and relatively easy-to-learn platform that will open up the world of robots, sensors, and computer-controlled Internet of Things to the relative novice. Some learning is required here, but it is a truly power device, and even Radio Shack now carries Arduino boards.

COMMUNITY COLLEGES

Jim Newton used to teach a "combat robotics" class at a junior college in California. He did it so that he could have access to the school's machine shop. He would show up as early as he could, often an hour before class, and stay long after the class was over, to work on his projects. Then a funny thing happened. He let his students know that he didn't mind if they wanted to stay late or come early. Many did. The following semester, some of the students came back. They already had robots, so Jim let them work on their projects, and then the following semester almost no one who signed up for the class was actually working on the class material.

It was a nice little hack to get access to the tools in the community college. Eventually, the school shut this program down. As they say, no good deed goes unpunished. Take the woodworking, metalworking, or electronics class at your local community college or continuing education program at a local university. See what you can make. Jim's need for access to these kinds of tools led him to build TechShop.

HACKERSPACE

Join or set up a hackerspace. These have sprung up around the world. Hackerspaces.org has basic instructions on how to set one up. Be careful though. There are some liability issues some of these spaces are ignoring, specifically, general liability and instructor liability insurance. It turns out that if an instructor teaches welding wrong and a student goes out and burns a building down or hurts someone, the instructor could be personally liable for damages, as could the hosting organization.

Hackerspaces have to carry instructor liability insurance, and it is not cheap. If the space can be tied in to a local educational institution, much of this can be mitigated, but not that many of the current spaces have that connection or the insurance. In their passion to get something done, they have just gone out and done it. This is laudable, but it can be very risky. Do your homework first. If you can find the right space and get the insurance, it is a great hobby.

PERSONAL STORY

A few years ago, I was running out of time to buy my wife a Valentine's Day present. Like a typical guy, I had waited until the last minute. I had to get to the airport quickly if I was even going to get home that night. I wasn't sure how good a Valentine's gift I would find at the airport. So I decided to make something. Quickly. Thankfully, there are plenty of supplies and scraps floating around our store, and I was able to find some red plastic sheets perfect for cutting with the laser cutter.

I went on the Internet and found a line art version of a rose, downloaded it, and then modified it to give it a little more style and panache. I reworked the design so that our laser cutter would cut it. Had I been thinking, I would also have cut out a stand. Fortunately, there was a break in the reservations at the laser cutter, and I jumped on. I added a nice "I love you" sentiment, a nickname, and I cut it. It worked on my first try. It only took about 20 minutes to make and left me with 20 minutes to spare at the airport. Just enough time to find a blank card to go with the gift.

That night when I got home and gave my wife her Valentine's gift, I was a hero. Lesson learned—again. Something I make and imbue with meaning is more touching than dozens of roses, pounds of chocolate, or fancy dinners. She still has that little piece of red plastic set up with her other most meaningful mementos.

This is one revolution that you will want to join. It doesn't just change you, it has the power to change those around you as well.

Conclusion

We are standing on the foundation of the largest explosion of creativity, knowledge creation, and innovation in all of human history. We do stand on the shoulders of the greats. We are surrounded by a cloud of witnesses who wait to see what we will do in the next 10 to 20 years of profound innovation. Call it what you will, the next industrial revolution, the Maker Movement, the creative revolution, the third industrial revolution, whatever you like. History will name it once it is over. The real question is, what are you going to do?

I am calling on you to join us. There are a lot of different ways to participate. You can start your own maker journey this week. Make something for someone else and then give it to him or her. The experience will change both you and the recipient. And you will begin to see the power of connecting with your inner maker.

I am also asking you to become a soldier or radical, if you will, and help with the movement overall. Makers need lots of help. Our message is really just beginning to get out. There are enormous political, social, educational, and structural things that need to change to fully leverage the movement. I'm confident that nothing is going to get in its way and that eventually it will become the massive force for creativity around the globe it deserves to become.

The real question, is how much time is it going to take? Everett Rogers in his famous work *Diffusion of Innovations* identified the process and amount of time a major innovation takes to be adopted. Across multiple domains and various innovations he discovered the basic outlines of how innovations diffuse into a target population. He also showed that they generally take a full 25 years to work their way fully into the lives of that target population. I was at a symposium recently where it was postulated that because of modern communication methods, Google, and the Internet, the rate of innovation diffusion may be increasing. There were no data offered, just a postulation. The key thing that you can do to help is to try to increase the speed with which Maker Movement ideas are spread. We really should not have to wait 25 years in this day and age for a movement this important to spread.

TRENDS

We live in an age where everything is changing more quickly than ever. The rate of change is literally speeding up. I owe my friends at Singularity University (SU) at NASA Ames for helping me to understand this better. Ray Kurzweil's book *The Singularity Is Near* is the basis of SU.[1] What he and they show is that a stunning number of technologies and trends are on a hypergrowth curve. Technically, the curve is logarithmic, a steady doubling of capability over a certain period of time. Moore's law is the most famous of the curves, but Ray points out many, many more. A result of the convergence of many of these stunning curves is that technology is growing at an exponential rate. Everyone is familiar with information technology; less understood is the biotech, nanotech, screen technology, genetics, and other areas that are seeing this kind of exponential growth.

As humans, we are not really wired to understand non-linear growth rates. We have a hard time planning for them, leveraging them, understanding them, or imagining a future impacted by them. The SU curriculum and experience is designed to help people begin to think exponentially.

When you combine these authors' ideas concerning technology change with technology access through open software, open hardware, software incubator, and makerspaces along with an exponential increase in the number of people who will have access to the tools needed to help drive innovation across multiple industries, you begin to see infinite possibilities.

POLICY

The policy implications of the Maker Movement and non-linear technological improvements are huge. If we believe in manufacturing as an important component in an economy, then the distribution and diffusion of easy-to-use, powerful, and cheap access to the right tools are critical to the success of every industrialized economy, particularly ones that want to leverage the coming technological advances across so many industries. Waiting for the markets and general social awareness to build the movement naturally and organically organize around this new world does not serve policy or humanity very well. The desired future can be reached more quickly with careful investment and thoughtful intervention in the right sectors.

There are multiple multibillion-dollar efforts underway in the United States to try to accelerate energy, cleantech, biotech, nanotech, and advanced manufacturing. For that same kind of money, we could build a thousand makerspaces and put one to two million of our most creative minds to work in their spare time. Or we could direct libraries to spend some of their grant money on supporting makerspace memberships. Some writers have suggested cohosting spaces with libraries. This is an interesting idea that might lead to more library fires from welders and laser cutters, so I'm not very excited about putting a full makerspace in a library. But it could work with the right planning and design, and access is the most important attribute of a makerspace. This attitude and approach is similar to a library's.

The entire educational system in the United States is outdated—built for a world that no longer exists, in a world that is continuing to change very rapidly. We have an incredible opportunity—and responsibility—to explore what education means in a fully networked, Internet-enabled, and makerspace–fueled world. Creating innovators and technology entrepreneurs should be one of education's top priorities.

The U.S. government should have a Maker Corps. Like the other corps, AmeriCorps and the Peace Corps, it would be a government-funded effort to help our best, brightest, and most creative change the world through meeting real-world needs with a combination of access to raw materials, makerspaces, and communities in need. It could be deployed after natural disasters; makers could show up with containers full of material, equipment, hands, education, and training.

I'm sure you can come up with at least a half a dozen of your own ideas. You should.

RESULTS

Buried in this manifesto are a lot very cool, fun, and often powerful inventions. Just to remind you of some of them, and maybe introduce you to a couple that I didn't describe earlier, these are the types of projects that can come out of makerspaces in your community once the makerspaces are built:

a desktop diamond manufacturing device, a fusion reactor, bamboo jewelry, the world's cheapest drip irrigation system, a GPS-enabled nitrogen detection device, Square, DODOcase, SFMade, Type A Machines, the world's fastest electric motorcycle, the world's most efficient data cooling center, a CubeSat miniature satellite, a 3D printer, a jet pack, fashion week competitors, carbon fiber guitars, world-class cellos, the Lumio lamp, a folding kayak, the C-Loop camera strap mount, the Oona smartphone stand, Better Off Wed cake toppers, Hugalopes, One Degree Watches, the Giraffe remote-controlled videoconference telepresence robots, ProtoTank hardware prototyping group, Driptech, and many, many more.

As more of the tools of manufacturing become available, as they get easier to use and more affordable, more and more people will gain access to them. As this continues to happen, an explosion in new innovative hardware ideas will develop and spread around the world. As the Internet gets hooked up to more devices, sensors, robots, switches, and controls and creates the Internet of Things, the opportunity for creating labor-saving devices, sensors that can reduce injury, tell us of impending failure, or even fix themselves, our lives will change and improve.

FINALLY

Each evening in makerspaces across the United States, the most inventive, creative, focused, and entrepreneurial people in any given city get together to learn, meet, teach, and make. They hang out in the open space and swap ideas. They help one another on their projects, art, and products. They learn from one another how to use new tools in new ways. They take classes, host events, attend meetings, and pick up new skills. They make new friends, find business partners, discover new customers, hire new employees, and get or create jobs. These spaces become the highest concentration of a multitalented cross section of the creative class ever assembled in each city. It becomes the aggregator of the best hardware-focused ideas in the city. It becomes a cathedral of creativity. All it is missing is you.

Let me finish with an invitation to come on out and take a free tour of one of our shop locations. These are friendly places, and we like to share. But be ready at the end of the tour for our basic question: What do you want to make? And be ready to develop into a new version of you, because answering that question could change your life or even the world.

Notes

Chapter 1

1. In a chapter called "Failing Free" in his book *Here Comes Everybody*, Clay Shirky focuses on open source software and self-organizing online social phenomena wherein experimentation is fostered in such a way that inventors fail fast and, resultantly, succeed faster. I'm extending the idea to include the physical world, as the inputs to production, labor, and capital (equipment and resources) can now be acquired with the equivalent of disposable income. From a macroeconomic perspective, moving money from leisure pursuits to innovative investments makes the resultant inventions free.

2. Steven Wheelwright and Kim B. Clark, *Revolutionizing Product Development* (New York: The Free Press, 1992), p. 22.

Chapter 4

1. Erik Brynjolfsson, Yu (Jeffrey) Hu, Michael D. Smith, "The Longer Tail: The Changing Shape of Amazon's Sales Distribution Curve," September 2010, p. 10. Social Science Research Network. ssrn.com/abstract=1679991.

2. Chris Anderson, "The Long Tail," *Wired* October 2004. Available at the *Wired* archive, http://www.wired.com/archive/12.10/tail.html.

3. Chris Anderson, *The Long Tail: Why the Future of Business Is Selling Less of More* (New York: Hyperion, 2006, revised edition 2008).

Chapter 5

1. Eric Von Hippel, *Democratizing Innovation* (Cambridge, MA: The MIT Press, 2006).
2. Henry Chesbrough, *Open Innovation: The New Imperative for Creating And Profiting from Technology* (Cambridge, MA: Harvard Business Review Press, 2003).
3. Alan Patricof, "Bring Back the Small Cap IPO," *CNN Money*, September 4, 2012, http://finance.fortune.cnn.com/2012/09/05/small-cap-ipo-market/.

Chapter 6

1. http://longnow.org/seminars/02013/feb/19/makers-revolution.

Chapter 7

1. http://techcrunch.com/2009/12/01/square-worth-40-million-before-launch/.
2. http://www.datacenterknowledge.com/archives/2011/12/12/clustered-systems-cools-100kw-in-single-rack/

Chapter 8

1. http://www.fastcompany.com/1645295/printable-brick-could-cut-worlds-carbon-emissions-least-800-million-tons-year-updated.

Chapter 10

http://www.ted.com/talks/gever_tulley_on_5_dangerous_things_for_kids.html.

Conclusion

1. Ray Kurzweil, *The Singularity Is Near* (New York: Penguin Group, 2005).

Index

About the Author

Mark Hatch, CEO and cofounder of TechShop, is a former Green Beret and has held executive positions focused on innovation, disruptive technology, and entrepreneurship at large and small firms alike. At Avery Dennison he launched Avery.com and then helped to drive global technology business development; at Kinko's, he launched the eCommerce portion of Kinkos.com and ran the computer services section inside Kinko's stores across the United States; and as the COO of Health Net's health benefits ASP, Mark helped to launch one of the early integrated health benefits portals.

A recognized leader in the global maker movement and a sought-after speaker and consultant on innovation, advanced manufacturing and leadership, Mark has spoken to groups from GE, Ford, P&G, ExxonMobile, Kraft, and other Fortune 500 firms. He has presented at universities like UC Berkeley and Harvard, as well as events such as TEDx, The Clinton Global Initiative, the Council on Foreign Relations, and Singularity U.

Mark has appeared on *ABC, CBS, NBC, PBS, Bloomberg, CNN*, and *Fox*, among others. He has been quoted in publications, including *Bloomberg Business, FastCompany, Inc, Forbes, The New York Times, The Wall Street Journal, The LA Times,*

The San Francisco Chronicle, and he has published a number of articles, including an opinion piece for the *Washington Post*.

Recently, *The San Francisco Business Times* presented Mark with a "Bay Area's Most Admired CEO Award." *Fast Company* has recognized him in its "Who's Next" column, and TechShop received the EXPY Award, given to the "experience stager of the year."

TechShop, a do-it-yourself workshop and fabrication studio with six locations open and hundreds more planned over the next decade, is the largest public access tools and computer enabled manufacturing platform in the world. Through TechShop, Mark is focused on radically democratizing access to the tools of innovation by providing the lowest cost access to tools the world has ever seen. With partners like Autodesk, Ford, GE, and Lowe's, along with governmental agencies like DARPA (for advanced manufacturing) and the Veterans Administration (for veteran training), TechShop is poised to help reshape how the world does innovation and manufacturing and has already begun to have a significant impact on the economic development opportunities in the communities where it is built.

Mark holds an M.B.A. from the Drucker Center at the Claremont Graduate University and a B.A. in Economics from the University of California at Irvine.